LEADERSHIP ATTITUDE

HOW MINDSET AND ACTION CAN CHANGE YOUR WORLD

Sonia
M C D O N A L D

CEO & Founder of LeadershipHQ

Testimonials

"When a woman as obsessed and mindful about leadership as Sonia McDonald has enough time to ponder and start typing – beware! Sonia's knowledge of leadership should be compulsory reading for government figures, top senior executives, line managers, or simply anyone wondering how to be a better leader. Here comes a book that will expand your mind and propel you to reconsider what you think you know about leadership."
– Derin Cag: Founder of Richtopia

"What a fabulous book! I have known Sonia for 15 years and her quest to learn and share is virtually unparalleled – and is truly represented by this book. *Leadership Attitude* is a must read for all leaders – it is full of great tips and is an easy read. Highly recommended!"
– Anna-Lucia Mackay: Educator, speaker and best-selling author
   of *The Four Mindsets*

"This book is amazing! It is a practical guide to building your personal leadership brand, without the painful mistakes made by trying to figure it out on your own! I found it inspirational and truly informative. I wish I had read this book 20 years ago. But it's never too late!"
– Tabitha Pearson: Chief Human Resources Officer,
   Super Retail Group

"Think you can't be a leader? Think again. Sonia McDonald uses some amazingly powerful and personal stories to help you connect with what it means to be a leader. You don't have to be in a position of leadership to lead but you do need the right attitude. Sonia and her book can help you with that."
– Anthony Campbell: Director, coach, mentor at
  Campbell Leadership Solutions

"Sonia's book brings refreshing clarity to many of the questions around what makes an effective leader. It's the kind of book that can and should be referred to time and again, providing practical, well-researched tips and tools based on Sonia's own extensive knowledge and experience. It's a perfect read for when you need a reality check on what it takes to be a good leader. Great for that plane trip too – when you need a refresher on all things leadership!"
– Samantha Kennerley: Chief Executive Officer, Youngcare

"Leadership is written about and discussed globally; in fact over 500,000 books have been published alone in the US. What Sonia has done with her book is cut through the noise and give readers insight based on authentically real stories."
– Jo Burston: Founder and CEO, Job Capital and Rare Birds

"Sonia McDonald is able to combine her insights into her own leadership journey with what's relevant and current in this space through exquisite writings and projects. I am impressed by Sonia's drive and passion for leadership and how graciously she articulates what leadership is about in this new era of work."
– Silvia Damiano: CEO & Founder, About my Brain Institute

"A great read. Clear concepts in an easy-to-read format, which reflect Sonia's upbeat, passionate personality!"
– Rachael Pogson: VP, Global Talent Acquisition & HR Central
  at Seagate Technology

"Leadership can be a tricky thing. We need more books that cut through the leadership jargon. Sonia has written one. I'd strongly advise reading it closely!"
– David Pich: Chief Executive – Membership,
   Australian Institute of Management

"If you want to access the key aspects of leadership quickly you should buy this book. It is practical, full of good advice, with so many handy tips, and it's clearly written for time poor professionals. Be prepared to be challenged to change, develop a leadership attitude and become the best you can be."
– Peter Little: Deputy Vice Chancellor
   (Corporate Programs and Partnerships), QUT

"Looking to be a stronger, more passionate leader? This book is totally for you. Dripping with inspiration, compelling research, practical how-to tips and rich examples, this is a must-read for leaders and those who will be one day. A refreshing and truly powerful read."
– Cath Nolan: Gender Gap Gone

"Leadership Attitude is a powerful handbook for every aspiring and current business leader. Sonia McDonald shifts the paradigm for what is true leadership and challenges the status quo with this easy to read and inspiring book. Highly recommended."
– Kylie Hammond: Chairman & CEO, Director Institute

"Sonia McDonald has stripped away some of the hype around 'leadership' with a refreshingly honest take on what is important for today's leaders. Inspiring yet practical, this book is Sonia McDonald in text."
– John Knight: Managing Director, businessDEPOT

"An inspiring, practical and brilliant book – one which will give you insights into the who, what and how of great leadership. Sonia establishes that attitude and action are a winning combination!"
– Beata Koropatwa: CEO, Auslaser Business Solutions & Chair,
    The Confidante P/L

"An inspiring book full of great stories and anecdotes about leadership. Sonia McDonald proves that attitude and action really do matter!"
– Kasia Gospos: Founder & CEO, LEADERS IN HEELS

"Let's be honest, there are a lot of books on leadership and I've read most of them – but Sonia McDonald has written one that is so fresh, energetic and thought-provoking that I loved every page. Sonia asks the big questions, the little questions and everything in between in such an authentic and honest way. Seriously, any leader who didn't learn a great deal about themselves and how they lead their teams from reading this book should probably re-think their chosen career."
– Andrew Griffiths: International bestselling business author, global speaker and media commentator

"Love this book. It's not just about leadership, it's about being YOU, and providing tools to guide you to be the best you can be. Well worth the read, and you'll keep coming back to it, like your own personal coach, time and time again."
– Nicola Mills: Group Managing Director, Pacific Retail

To my darling daughter, Abby,
I am so proud, and I love you with all my heart.

To my parents, June and Alex, I am forever grateful
for you always being there and love you both dearly.

To my best friend, Maria, thank you
for being my rock and caring so much for me.

First published in 2016 by
LeadershipHQ
www.leadershiphq.com.au

National Library of Australia Cataloguing-in-Publication entry
Author: Sonia McDonald
Title: Leadership Attitude – How mindset and action can change your world
ISBN: 978-0-9946452-0-3
Subjects: Leadership. Industrial management. Self-actualisation.
Dewey No. 158.4

Editing, book cover design and formatting services by BevRyanPublishing.com

Disclaimer:
Any information in the book is purely the opinion of the author based on her personal experience and should not be taken as business or legal advice. All material is provided for educational purposes only. We recommend to always seek the advice of a qualified professional before making any decision regarding personal and business needs.

Contents

About the Author – Sonia McDonald

Sonia McDonald is CEO and Founder of LeadershipHQ, a team of specialist consultants with over 30 years' experience in organisational and leadership development, who have helped companies successfully complete multi-million dollar projects and build exceptional leaders and cultures.

Sonia is one of Australia's leading executive leadership coaches, as well as an inspirational keynote speaker. She has a business degree in human resources and psychology, as well as a Diploma in Neuroscience, and has worked internationally in the people and culture space within a number of different industries.

Sonia has spoken on leadership, neuroscience, entrepreneurship, confidence and attitude, as well as diversity at numerous events, conferences, and summits around the world.

With a true passion for working with people and helping them be the best they can be, Sonia has been recognised as one of the 'Top 250 Influential Women Across the Globe' by *Richtopia*.

In 2015 she launched an online magazine, *LeadershipHQ*, which showcases leaders, leadership, and entrepreneurs. She is also the author of the *Neuroscience of Leadership* Kindle book, available on Amazon.

1

Her LeadershipHQ blog has been named in 'Australia's Fastest Growing Careers and 50 Best Job Blogs' and was recently listed in the 'Top 100 Leadership Blogs' across the globe. She believes that good leadership can change lives.

Sonia has also been published in *The Australian, HRD Magazine, Business Insider, Business Woman's Media, Style Magazine, Richtopia, Smart Healthy Women, Business Chicks,* and *Women in Focus.*

Sonia is deeply committed to working with organisations, teams, and leaders to build their leadership capability and mindset, and she brings an energetic, authentic, and passionate attitude to everything she does.

Find out more about Sonia McDonald and LeadershipHQ at www.soniamcdonald.com.au or www.leadershiphq.com.au

Acknowledgements

I never thought I would be where I am today. But where I am is definitely where I need to be. We all are. Writing this book has been such a dream for me, with some incredible learnings along the way. Building an entire company from a blog has been the best and the most challenging thing I have ever done.

Over the years I have had many amazing successes as well as heartbreaking challenges. It is the incredible people and tribe around me that have made the difference to me and our success and significance. I am blessed beyond belief and I adore every single one of you for being there, cheering me on, and helping me be the best I can be. I thank you for caring about me and ultimately for my daughter Abby, too.

To my beautiful, funny, and talented daughter Abby: I do what I do for you. You are the reason I started this company. You are the reason I wrote this book. You inspire me every day. You are exceptional and talented. I know you have an incredible future ahead of you. I wanted to show you that if I can do this, you can do it too. I am proud and blessed to have a daughter who is so kind, loving, and supportive. I know there have been times where things have been challenging. You have always been there and understood my purpose and what we were trying to achieve.

Thank you for being you and always standing up for me, too. You are my greatest cheerleader.

To my darling family: Thank you to my incredible mum and dad, June and Alex, my sister Natalie, and my brother Conrad for all your support and love. It means the world to me.

To my incredibly talented team: Chauntelle, Anne, Geoff, Kim, Megan, Rachael, Tony, Julie and Rachel; you all *rock*! You have been there through the greatest and toughest of times. You have always wanted the best for me and LeadershipHQ. You have told me exactly what you think and gone above and beyond to help me be the best I can be. Thank you for all your dedication and commitment over the years. I would not be where I am today without you.

To my brilliant mentors: Over the years I have been honoured and blessed to have a number of people who have mentored, coached, and supported me. You have never asked for anything in return. Thank you, John; I met you a number of years ago and you were an unexpected light in my life – thank you with all my heart. Thank you Peter; you have always cared about my vision and purpose, and ensured I stayed focused. Thank you, Stephen; your innovative and open mind blows me away – thank you for being an inspiration to me. Thank you, Grant for your openness, and incredibly direct and constructive feedback. Thank you, Kylie; your generosity, incredible entrepreneurial mind, and support have meant the world to me. Thank you, Amelia; your massive heart, integrity and drive have been an inspiration to me. Thank you Carolyn, Megan, Greg, Beata, Tim, Michael and Ted for the amazing ways you have helped me look at the world and helped me to be the best I can be, without any expectations. Thank you Mark for introducing me to the amazing world of leadership and consulting. You are all beyond brilliant.

To my beautiful tribe: My tribe means the world to me as you give me the strength to keep moving forward; you are always there and are amazing human beings. Your love and friendship has meant the world to me over the years, and I am truly blessed to have so many incredible and generous people in my life. Thank you Maria, Shelley, Jo, Tamlyn, Carolyne, Eveline, and Matthew – my dearest friends who have been in my life forever. I love you all dearly.

To my amazing LeadershipHQ Leaders and Community: The LeadershipHQ journey has been built from so much passion, tenacity, vision, and a lot of learnings. I am thrilled to be sharing this book with you. It has been *you* that has made a difference to my vision and purpose. I am blessed to have worked with and coached so many incredible leaders and clients who are dedicated to making a difference in leadership. Thank you for your commitment and dedication to being the best you can be by reading this book, the blogs, and magazine. Leadership is always about self-development. Thank you for contributing to the world of leadership and the LeadershipHQ Community. I wrote this book for you; for you to see how you can be a leader, as it is all about attitude. Remember, we lead our world and we can all make a difference.

Finally, I want to add a special thank you to Bev Ryan and Anne Maybus for your help and support with this book.

Introduction

I choose my attitude. I choose a leadership attitude.

I googled leadership today, as I write this in December 2015, and found 634,000,000 results. I actually needed to take a deep breath. Breath taken. Now, let's talk about leadership. Have we made leadership bigger than it is? Yes, I think so. Look at those results!

So why I am writing a book? There is a story here, can you sense it?

I call myself the Accidental Entrepreneur as well as a semi-expert in leadership. Why accidental? Well, looking back on my life, I never expected to be where I am now. But I am exactly where I need to be. An entrepreneur.

I remember being maybe five years old and I had just started grade 1. I was waiting at the gate for my very patient mother to pick me up from school and I saw a group of children getting onto a bus. I thought to myself, "I wonder where they are going?" and it looked like fun, so I walked over and got on the bus as well. I could see my mother running down the pathway looking for me as I waved out the window. She didn't see me but I thought she would find me eventually. I stayed on the bus until it reached the end of its journey and the bus driver said, "Where were you supposed to get off?" I replied, "Nowhere. I came for the ride." I didn't realise it then, but this was the start of me finding out that I am pretty fearless and adventurous – and a pain in the butt. It's my first memory of either being a real brat or starting on my path to being an entrepreneur.

I now lead a growing leadership consulting business and you could call me CEO, managing director, business owner, or founder. They are all great titles. I would call myself a leader – and a semi-expert at that. Why? The leader title will be explained in this book. The semi-expert is because I never want to stop learning about leadership and myself. I feel if I call myself an expert, my brain will say, "That's it, you don't need to know any more."

I am essentially writing this book for my younger self. What would you say to yourself if you could go back in time? Party more … or party less? Listen to your parents? Study harder at school? Mine would be to learn leadership and start now!

My leadership journey started over a decade ago. At least the part I am aware of did. If I look back at school, university, and early on in my career, I am sure I could think of examples where I was a leader and entrepreneur. And by the way, we all can!

However, a decade ago, I had a very unexpected start to my focus on leadership. I have always loved people and I knew since I was young that I wanted to work with people. I've also loved to write since I was little, hence my passion for writing blogs, articles, our magazine, and now this book.

My degree and background are in human resources with some senior and not-so-senior roles across the globe. In my early 30s

I decided to put my career on hold and have a baby – and focus on my husband's career. We had moved to Shanghai, China when Abby, our daughter, was about 18 months old. Truly I thought moving to China and being an expat wife would be a lot of fun, and easy. It was the opposite. It was hard living in a foreign country – and I got bored. I landed a great part-time role for a global search firm. I loved it. Then my world fell apart. It was completely unexpected and devastating. It was here I learnt about true resilience.

I finally moved back to Australia as a single parent, and had no idea what to do. I tried staying with the company I worked for, as they were incredibly supportive, but the travel and role demanded more time away from Abby. I had to walk away. I had to reinvent myself.

I did that by opening myself up to opportunities. I put myself out there. I met someone who worked in the leadership space and he asked if I knew about leadership as he had a consulting gig open in his company. I looked at him and said "Yes, absolutely." I was freaking out, to be honest, and remember thinking, please don't ask me any questions as I really don't know that much. I totally *faked it!* Okay, I had some knowledge as I do have a degree in business and I wasn't faking brain surgery. I got the job! I raced home and bought every single leadership book I could. I researched, read, and lived and breathed leadership.

I started working with engineering and construction companies – and major construction projects across Queensland. I loved it. It was awesome. I was finally making a difference. I found my passion. I found my purpose. I love to write, and I decided to tap back into that. I also love to teach. So I had found this great niche. Writing and teaching. I started a blog called LeadershipHQ – Leadership Headquarters – and discovered over a few years that I had quite a following. How cool. Then a few people around me encouraged me to start my own business. I would literally glare at them and say, "Are you crazy? That is way too scary." It planted a seed though.

I became the flipchart queen. You know that flipchart paper that looks like gigantic Post-it notes? I had flipcharts all over the walls at my home office for a *year*! I would write down ideas, insights, products, services, websites, brands, marketing, strategy ... everything I could think of to turn the blog into a company. Then I did it. After a year, I jumped off the cliff. I started my own leadership business. I only wish I had done it earlier. I had a great attitude; I knew I could do it.

This book is one of the most important things I have ever embarked on. Trust me, writing a book is scary stuff. I love to write. I write articles and blogs, created an e-magazine, and publishing a book seemed like a natural next step. Until it has taken me two years to write it! Give me a break; I have had a lot on!

I am the leader of a leadership consulting firm. I don't have a PhD or an MBA, nor am I working for a university or institution that researches leadership. This book is essentially my insights, knowledge, and thoughts from over 10 years working in leadership – and it is about making a difference in how you see yourself. We all lead our world, and my purpose is to build a world of future leaders.

Perception changes everything. I never saw myself as a leader until I changed my reality. Now I am a leader. I make a difference.

Leadership is such a huge and fundamental part of my life. I read, research, teach, and coach this stuff every day. I am beyond passionate about it. This book is about my key insights and learnings that are empowering, practical, and fun. This book shares everything I know about 'you' as a leader, people leadership, and leadership as a whole.

When you read through this book, link the learnings back to yourself and consider how you can put them into action. I read a lot and always write the key insights from each chapter at the start of my book. I do this so when I refer back to it, I know what resonated with me.

In this book, I have also created some spaces for you to reflect, write, and answer some questions, too. Pretty cool! Make sure you spend some time doing this; it will help you learn, change, and *grow*.

Now, what would I tell my younger leadership self?

I think about this question every day. Why? Because I would tell her many different things. In a nutshell:

- Start now. Leadership matters.

- Have the *best* leadership attitude every day. You choose your attitude.

- Learn and open yourself to who you truly are. This self-discovery journey never ends.

- Pick up a leadership book and start reading it. I would personally read this one cover to cover, but I also mention several others throughout this book.

- Be authentic. The best leaders are those who know that self-awareness is the greatest capability.

- Integrity is central to leadership. Lead by example.

- Focus on getting to know yourself – self-awareness is the key.

- The best leaders own their story. It does not define you, but your story makes you who you are.

- Take more risks. Say *yes* to opportunities! Just jump. Act now.

- Own what makes *you* different. Own it. You rock!

- Trust your natural ability – you can do it.

- Believe in yourself – confidence rocks. Trust yourself. Put your hand up!

- Don't take *no* for an answer. If they say no, go to the next. Find that *yes*.

- Surround yourself with empowering people who lift you higher. Your tribe. Your cheerleaders. Get rid of people who put holes in your rowboat.

- Give more to others. Mentor and coach others. If you are successful, don't forget to send the elevator down for others to ride up in.

- Empower others to lead. Leadership is about others.

- Be compassionate and curious. Be kind to yourself first and then to others.

- Network! Meet as many people as you can. Add value to them.

- Never stop learning. Invest in yourself. Only you matter.

- Enjoy your amazing ride. It is incredible. Take in your leadership journey.

It's an Attitude

You know what? I always saw leadership as a role or title. Many of us do. But it is not about your role, position, or title. I have met many people who have assumed that title or role but who are not leaders. I have also met lots of people who don't have a leadership position or role but who are leaders. Leadership can also take many forms; as a parent, coach, role model, and team member!

Leadership. It is an attitude. It is how you think, feel, and see yourself and how you act as a leader. It is about being the leader you want to be.

Leadership is an attitude.

If I can do it, YOU CAN!

Chapter 1

Leadership is an Attitude

Leadership. If there is one thing I would tell my younger self, it's to start learning leadership *now*. Start *now*.

I had it in me, but didn't see, feel, or think it. And guess what? We all have it in us. It is up to you to change your attitude.

Leadership makes the difference. Attitude is more important than ability, and it determines altitude. (Thanks Zig Ziglar!)

A few months ago I was standing in front of a group of about 200 university students, about to speak to them about leadership attitude and confidence. I asked them who saw themselves as a leader. I wasn't surprised when hardly anyone put up his or her hand. We see this often, whether it is a group of students or team of executives.

> **Attitude, not aptitude determines altitude.**
> – Zig Ziglar

Okay, I get it; putting your hand up in front a group of people is a little daunting so maybe a few might have thought they were leaders – just not prepared to admit it! Thing is, I ask this of every group of leaders that I speak to, coach, or work with. They don't put up their hands – or very few do. Why? Have we made leadership more complex or bigger than what it is?

Do we think of leadership as a role or a title? Do you need the word 'manager' or 'leader' in your title to think of yourself as a leader? It is *not* about role or title. We can all be leaders. We are all leaders. It is about *attitude*! It is a mindset. It is how you see yourself. You are a leader. If you don't see yourself as a leader – *yet* – keep reading this book!

Attitude matters! Attitude reflects leadership!

Why? Guess what? If you don't see yourself as a leader, you are not one. As Henry Ford once said, "If you think you can't, you can't". If you start to see yourself as a leader, you will be one. *Yes*, I hear you saying, *really*? Or maybe even, *bring it on*!

Think about this. How would it feel to be the leader you want to be; to inspire, to influence, to lead with vision and purpose, to make a difference, to truly understand yourself and others, to lead change, and to coach and mentor? Okay, that seems like a long list and I could go on. I am not saying you have to do or be all of that to be a leader. You could, though. How would it feel if you could lead; truly lead? Lead like the true leader you are? It starts with you. Your mindset and attitude. Believe it and you will become it.

Attitude is a little thing that makes a big difference.

— Winston Churchill

It starts with you. And leadership can be learnt. Absolutely it can!

The thing about attitude is that it turns into behaviours and actions. If your attitude says 'I am a leader', then it will come out in your actions!

Leadership isn't about position. It's about attitude and how you act. It is about behaviour and action.

Let me share this wonderful story. I remember being asked to coach a superintendent on a major construction site. He was seen as a legend in the construction world with over 45 years' technical experience, and had been brought up on the tools. I walked into his office and he literally looked like Santa Claus with the big long white beard. I could tell immediately he wasn't interested in working with me. And I got it. I wouldn't either if I were in his shoes. This 40-year-old blonde woman coming onto his site and coaching him on leadership? Come on! So I sat. We stared at each other. I smiled. I looked around the room and noticed he had some books on leadership on his shelf. My eyes literally lit up. So I asked him, "What does leadership mean to you and do you see yourself as a leader?" He told me rather abruptly that no, he didn't see himself as a leader.

There was this eerie silence. I replied, "I see some books on leadership on your shelf. Is there an interest?" He said yes. It was at that moment I knew I could make a difference. His mind was open to it. Despite his gruff demeanour, he was open to learning and he had opened his mind to leadership. On my journey with him, what changed was his attitude and thinking. He was brought up thinking leadership was about authority, title, and where you stood in the organisational structure. When I changed his leadership attitude and mindset, he changed how he saw himself. He saw himself as a leader. He had the leadership attitude, and he made such a difference to that project.

It is how you feel about leadership and yourself. Now let's talk about *you* in the next chapter.

What is your attitude about leadership? Today, I want you to see and believe you are a leader!

> Some people want it to happen, some wish it would happen, others make it happen.
> — Michael Jordan

GREAT TIPS ✔

- **Positive affirmations and attitude.**
  Nearly 90 per cent of our thoughts are negative. These thoughts are referred to as ANTs (Automatic Negative Thoughts), and they aren't good for us – we will discuss these in Chapter 8. You need to tell yourself "I am great" and "I am a strong leader".

- **Remind yourself.**
  We should keep reminding ourselves about all the good things we have ever accomplished or achieved.

- **Change your thinking.**
  Leadership is about attitude, mindset, and action. Not title.

- **You are in control.**
  Your attitude is your choice.

- **You are accountable.**
  You need to be accountable for your attitude and for your leadership.

START NOW

Chapter 2

Why Leadership?

One of my favourite exercises to do, and a pretty simple one at that, is to draw a line down the middle of a whiteboard and write 'management' on one side and 'leadership' on the other. Then I brainstorm with my groups about the differences between them.

Some of the words that come up are –

Leadership:
Vision, Integrity, Coach, Motivate, Trust, Respect, Influence

Management:
Organiser, Process, Direction, Plan, Rules

It is great to see what people come up with. When I ask them what words resonate with them around leadership, what they see in themselves and why leadership matters, you see the light

Those who lead inspire us ... Whether they are individuals or organisations, we follow those who lead not because we have to but because we want to.

– Simon Sinek

bulbs happening. Honestly, I see bulbs lighting up above their heads.

It's interesting that even without having consciously thought about the distinction, people can come up with these really important points. It's quite obvious to them that **leadership is about people,** where **management is about function.** And that's a vital distinction.

That's why many people can be born managers, but not everyone is a natural leader. As we grow, we're taught to look at processes, and follow the steps to get things done. It's neat. It's tidy. And it keeps us all in line.

When you start looking at people, the managers amongst us start to feel uncomfortable because there's no clear step-by-step plan for dealing with people. We're all seemingly unpredictable. And that's why leadership is so important.

You see, we're not really all that unpredictable. We all want to follow a true leader; someone who inspires us rather than directs us.

Leadership matters. It makes the difference. We all know that more often than not people leave their managers, not the organisation. Leadership matters a great deal to our organisations, to the people who work in them, and to the people who are served by them. For our community to function effectively, we need leaders who can encourage people to perform at their absolute best.

Becoming a great leader takes hard work. It is not very different to becoming a great athlete. To become great in any area, whether it is your career, your family, or within your community, you must use the unique strengths you were born with and develop them to their fullest potential, while acknowledging and learning from your shortcomings.

> *Champions aren't made in the gyms. Champions are made from something they have deep inside them – a desire, a dream, a vision.*
> — Muhammad Ali

When I reflect on leaders who have made a difference in my life, I can identify many who influenced why I came to work each day, how engaged I was, and even why I stayed with an organisation. I worked with some great leaders and I have worked for others who use the power of their position to do some really stupid things, the jerks! We have all worked with a jerk – the leader who controls, micromanages, yells and screams, takes credit for everything, says one thing and does another. Think about how different we feel at work when we have a great leader versus the jerk? It matters!

And we can learn leadership.

You know what? These jerks can destroy great people and great organisations. They then either move on or stay to witness their organisation steadily decline. We have all seen this. If you haven't, you will. Don't be the jerk; be the best leader you can be.

If you want to be a leader who can motivate, influence, and inspire others to do more and achieve success, it is essential that you discover who you are as a leader.

Also, if you are already in a leadership position, consider your need to keep pace with a workplace that is rapidly changing. Don't take it out on your team by exerting pressure on them. We just don't tolerate leaders who want to control, micromanage us, or lead with bullying! By the way, the brain does *not* like being micromanaged!

As Dr Rachel Cotter Davis, an American organisational development specialist, once said, "Your boss micromanaging you is like someone walking behind you in a dark alley in terms of what it does to the brain".

Great leaders, therefore, are people who can be trusted, who invest the time to explain the 'why' and who take others with them on the journey, inspiring and encouraging them to be the best they can be.

Simon Sinek wrote one of my favourite books, *Start with Why*. I love it because he links the *why* beautifully through a neuroscience lens. The *why* taps into the emotional part of the brain, the limbic system, the part of the brain that makes most of our decisions. Why do you *do* what you do? One of the best quotes from the book is, "People don't buy what you do, they buy why you do it."

As I said, people leave managers, not organisations. Talent stays with the company that offers great leadership and a sense of belonging. People want to be engaged and developed, and feel that they are part of something that is meaningful on many different levels. This is why the *why* is pivotal.

To be a leader, you need to be able to take people with you. People want the opportunity to develop themselves and do their best work. The options and opportunities open to workers today mean that people refuse to remain locked in negative situations.

A few years ago, I was working on a major construction site and coaching a number of leaders. One leader was new to a management role and he just didn't get the leadership space – or why he needed a coach.

I sat down with him and explored the why, what, and how of my work. He looked at me and said, "Are you like a personal trainer in leadership?" "Yes," I laughed. He looked at me and said, "I don't think I need this." I said, "Okay, but let's just give it a go." I have never worked with anyone (initially so resistant) who, after a few months, was so passionate, committed, and excited about leadership coaching. He was growing and changing, and he soon started coaching his own team.

If you are not the best leader you can be, you will not attract or retain the best people and they won't give you their best work.

What is your why? Why do you do what you do?

To an extent, leadership is like beauty: it's hard to define, but you know it when you see it.   — Warren Bennis, on becoming a leader

GREAT TIPS ✔

- **Which leadership words resonate with you?**
  Do the exercise I described at the start of this chapter, and write down words you associate with both 'leadership' and 'management'. Choose the words describing or meaning leadership, which you most prefer.

- **Think about why leadership matters to you.**

- **What is your why and purpose?**
  This might take time to reflect on – write your ideas down.

LEADERSHIP
can be
LEARNT!

Chapter 3

You *Rock*

I was sitting in my office organising one of my public leadership programs. I'd had 10 amazing women attending my program that week and I was reading through some of their 360 assessments. I was feeling very excited. Then I got to Rebecca's assessment and I was really surprised. Even though she'd been given some great feedback, some of the negative comments were rather harsh. She was called aggressive and very hard. I think someone might have called her a bulldog. Ugh!

I thought to myself that this was going to be an interesting program. What struck me like a lightning bolt was that in the program Rebecca was the opposite of her assessment – the very opposite.

I pulled her aside at morning tea, asked her how she felt about the feedback

> **Don't you ever let a soul in the world tell you that you can't be exactly who you are.**
>
> – Lady Gaga

(which she was given prior to the program), and discovered she was devastated. Two days into my program, after discovering who she really was as a leader, she burst into tears. She realised she had been someone other than herself. She then went back to work – and rocked it! She started being who she really is as a person and leader – and her world completely changed!

Don't be someone else – be you! Leadership is about you. *You*! We spend much of our lives being someone other than who we truly are. I get it. I truly do. But when we work with leaders and we hone in on who they are, their strengths and weaknesses (we are not perfect and that is totally cool), and what is unique about them as a leader, we see them truly shine. The greatest gift you can give yourself and others as a leader is being you. Being you means owning who you are and ultimately what makes you different and unique!

Leaders need to understand what makes them tick. Self-awareness and knowing who you are as a leader are the keys. Why? The better you know and understand yourself, the more you understand others. It will also help you understand what you have to offer that is special and different.

Leaders have a variety of talents, gifts, strengths, and styles and lead in many different ways. We each have our preferred method of leading, although we can probably change our style if the situation calls for something else. Leaders understand their preferred style. Leaders know why they rock. They know their purpose, values, and principles. They know what makes them tick – and also what can trip them up. I like to call them our triggers. Mine was that I really disliked failing (who doesn't!), but some leaders have a trigger about succeeding!

This self-awareness is a powerful grounding for becoming the leader you truly want to be – being authentic and real. Yes, I said the authentic and real you. No one else. Of course, when you think of leaders (good and bad) that have made a difference to you, they would have had an impact on who you are today.

> *If you deliberately plan on being less than you are capable of being, then I warn you that you'll be deeply unhappy for the rest of your life. You will be evading your own capabilities, your own possibilities.* — Maslow

Values Are a *Must* Have

> *What one does is what counts. Not what one had the intention of doing.*
> — Pablo Picasso

Know your values. Leaders are defined by their values as well as their actions. By leading by example, and leading with your values in a congruent and consistent way, you will bring meaning to your work and life.

As a leader, your actions are being watched. You demonstrate your values in everything you do. People around you are looking not only at the consistency and authenticity of your actions but also at the way you act and the choices you make.

We all have our own values. Organisations have values. Our individual team members have their values. It is important not only to know your values but theirs as well. Values drive what we do and how we all operate.

Although the values held by us are personal, integrity is the one value that is required in every leader. I call this the centre pole of leadership. You must exercise integrity in your leadership to gain people's trust, walk the talk, and lead by example. If other people cannot trust you, why would they want to work with you? Think about it: if you say one thing and do another, who would want to be led by you? The brain needs trust to be fully effective. When we see you as a foe, then we are not operating at an engaged and productive level.

What are your values? How can you put these into action?

Mine are passion, excellence, integrity, results, and partnership. I would love you to think about yours and write them down. You might have a few or a dozen, but it is important that you know them, why they are important, and how you will put them into action.

> *Your beliefs become your thoughts,*
> *Your thoughts become your words,*
> *Your words become your actions,*
> *Your actions become your habits,*
> *Your habits become your values,*
> *Your values become your destiny.*
> *– Mahatma Gandhi*

You Rock and Stand Out!

In becoming a great leader, there is little time to follow the herd or play it safe. Only people who stand out get a chance to show what they are really made of. As the German writer Goethe once said, "Boldness has genius, power and magic in it." Don't be afraid to be who you really are. That's what will make you different. Be honest and authentic, and allow people to know the real you. Guess what? We are not perfect; none of us are. Don't focus on what does *not* make you rock, for we all have weaknesses. Focus on what *makes* you rock. We all have our own special strengths and talents. Focus on your strengths and talents. Why? Because we have them for a reason. We will talk about strengths in the next chapter.

Focus on what makes you different, your values and self-awareness, be authentic and true to yourself – and focus on your strengths and talents. That's enough to distinguish you as a leader to be watched and followed.

Today you are YOU,
That is TRUER than true
There is NO ONE alive
Who is YOUER than YOU!
– Dr. Seuss

What Makes You Different and Unique?

Some find this a hard question to answer, but it is important to think about it and write it down. We have 7.3 billion different brains on this planet – and therefore 7.3 billion unique people who bring something different to our world. Own it. The chances are these are your key strengths, too. These are areas you can build on.

GREAT TIPS ✔

- **Find a self-awareness tool.**
  There are plenty – 360, Leadership Diagnostics and Psycho-metrics, or even just have conversations with people who can give you feedback.

- **Do the values exercise.**
  Google 'values exercise' and then sit down and spend time thinking about your values and why they are your values. Think about what they mean to you and how you can put them into action.

- **Write down a list of words about what makes you different and unique.**
  Now own it.

- **Authentic leader's reflection.**
  Grab a piece of paper, draw a line, and start to think about your life journey. The best leaders own and know their story. It is what has made you who you are today.

You ROCK!

Chapter 4

Emotional and Social Intelligence

I am sure you have all heard of IQ. I want to explore the notion of EQ – emotional intelligence. Don't run for the hills yet. Emotional intelligence is *vital* for a leader. The ability to understand your emotions, the emotions of others, resilience, relationship management, and social skills are all a part of emotional intelligence. I am sure you have all met those people that are super smart, technically brilliant, and can walk into a room and have *no* awareness of how they impact people. Here I would be thinking George from *Seinfeld* or even Mr. Smarty Pants in your physics class at University who got all distinctions and bragged about it, not caring how it affected others. Those people can drive us nuts! EQ matters!

In the *Harvard Business Review* article *What Makes a Leader*, Daniel Goleman discusses his research at nearly 200

If your emotional abilities aren't in hand, if you don't have self-awareness, if you are not able to manage your distressing emotions, if you can't have empathy and have effective relationships, then no matter how smart you are, you are not going to get very far.

– Daniel Goleman

large global companies, which showed that while the qualities tradi-
tionally associated with successful leadership – such as intelligence,
determination and vision – are required, they are not enough. Truly
great leaders also require a high degree of emotional intelligence,
including self-awareness, self-regulation, relationship management,
empathy, and social skills. Big time! Remember the brain is a social
organ – and it is important to learn EQ.

While you don't see it listed on a general job description for leaders,
it doesn't change the fact that emotional intelligence determines
our ability to manage ourselves and boosts our creativity on many
levels. And while a good IQ is necessary to move forward with
great strides, a high EQ is a strong predictor of leadership success.

Emotional Intelligence (EQ)

Emotional intelligence is made up of various components such as
self-awareness, self-management, relationship management, and
social awareness. It is easy to see, once broken down, how many
of these facets come into play on a daily basis in the workplace.

Self-Awareness

Self-awareness lies at the heart of emotional intelligence. Before
you can manage others, you must first understand yourself and
your motivations. What makes you happy, angry, frustrated, or
sad for starters? Understanding even the most basic of feelings
and their respective triggers will enable you to tune into someone
else's feelings more quickly.

Self-Management

Once you understand your feelings and triggers, i.e. what makes you sad or angry, then you can do your best to control how you respond to them. If a particular type of behaviour causes you to lose your temper, then you need to focus on defusing the anger before you do anything else. If your emotions challenge a situation, you must acknowledge and amend any kind of negativity at the outset.

Relationship Management

Being an effective leader revolves around being part of a team and collaborating with others. If people feel comfortable working with you, then it means you have developed an emotional connection with them. Trust plays a big part in creating a healthy and supportive group and will reward you in many situations.

Social Awareness

Social awareness is the next stepping stone to developing those relationships even further. If you are distracted or preoccupied to the point where you cannot listen or respond with empathy, then something needs to give. No one likes to feel ignored, especially when it comes from a position of authority. An empathetic person will, in turn, have more control and leverage over their team as a whole.

As you can see, emotional intelligence has a substantial impact on your leadership and business performance. Maintaining control of your EQ will differentiate you from those leaders who focus on IQ rather than connecting with their emotions. It will also promote many other benefits such as a boost in productivity and higher company morale.

Now For Social Intelligence ...

We have talked about EQ, and the concept of IQ is something we are familiar with. We understand that having smarts can advance our careers, and carry a project from start to finish, overcoming hurdles along the way. So let's now talk about social intelligence.

Having the capacity to understand not only our own emotions, but the emotions of those around us, as well as recognising and understanding emotional cues and reactions, is important when leading a team.

Although it is often viewed as interchangeable and confused with emotional intelligence, social intelligence is something else entirely. Being able to read and understand emotions is one thing and can, to some degree, be somewhat academic and 'text book'. You can teach people what facial expressions mean, and how to read body language.

Social intelligence takes this to the next level. Rather than simply reacting the appropriate way to a particular emotional cue, it is the empathy – the very real and very deep understanding of that emotion – which marks the difference between the two.

It also works both ways; a leader with high social intelligence will not only be able to feel, quite literally, the emotions of one of their team – they also understand that their actions have a profound impact on their team. It's all to do with brain chemistry and how humans, as social beings, interact and react to the emotions of those around them.

Leaders will have their actions and behaviours reflected back at them by their team. Upbeat, genuinely supportive and encouraging leaders will be blessed with a team of people who are more relaxed, less stressed, and who perform well. They feel confident in sharing ideas, and speaking up when things aren't going well.

In contrast, a leader who leads by dictating, and who is humourless and officious, is more likely to have a team who go through the motions; ticking off items on their to-do list, and keeping very much to themselves.

You can see that in a team environment, the latter fosters a culture of individualism, whereas the former cultivates a true team where everyone works together for the betterment of the project.

In effect, the more socially attuned you are to those around you, the more likely you are to be able to respond to them in a way that extracts the best from them – and your behaviours and attitudes will be reflected back at you by your team. Emotions are contagious, whether consciously or not, and can significantly influence those you're surrounded by and working with.

Even more exciting is that this mutual connectedness increases the social intelligence of both parties, strengthening the social neurons in the brains of both.

Just like all intelligence, some people are naturals and others need to work on improving theirs. Social intelligence is no different, and requires thoughtful actions to be taken in order to strengthen, or in some cases, develop it.

Forced and self-conscious social interactions are evident, and lack the authenticity required for genuine social connectedness. However, it is a good place to start practising and to develop your social intelligence. Keep in mind that social intelligence enhances brain development in both you, the leader, and those you deal with, so it's not only you who improves as you develop.

It is just one of the many reasons social intelligence *rocks*!

GREAT TIPS ✔

- **You can learn EQ.**
  Grab Daniel Goleman's book on the topic or read Harvard Business Review's *What Makes a Leader* by Daniel Goleman.

- **Do an EQ or SEI assessment and find a tool.**
  (SEI – Six Seconds Emotional Intelligence survey) If you are interested in finding out how you rate in these areas there are plenty of tools and assessments. A simple and effective one is the book *Emotional Intelligence 2.0*.

- **Think about a word that describes how you are feeling right now.**
  This is a great first step in building emotional intelligence. When we pay attention to how we're feeling, we learn to trust our emotions, and we become far more adept at managing them.

- **Take responsibility for your feelings and behaviour.**
  You own your feelings and your behaviours. No one else makes you feel or do something, so take responsibility for yourself.

- **Learn to respond instead of react.**
  When you react to something – a trigger or a prompt – you aren't in control of yourself. Stop reacting and start thinking about your actions. Learn to respond, which means making a conscious choice.

- **Surround yourself with positivity.**
  Positive vibes make you feel good, so it's great for your health, but it makes others feel good, too. A positive environment produces thriving people.

Self-Awareness is the KEY

Chapter 5

Play to Your Strengths

I have worked with and seen leaders, teams, and organisations truly transform by playing to their strengths.

However, 99 per cent of the leaders I work with want to work on their weaknesses. Maybe not 99 per cent but close enough. Why? Think about it; if I were to ask you to tell me about your weaknesses or your strengths, what would come to your mind immediately? Weaknesses? If not, congratulations, love your work! Believe me, it is much easier for the brain to focus on the negatives rather than what makes you rock. But you can change this.

> **Success is achieved by developing our strengths, not by eliminating our weaknesses.**
>
> – Marilyn vos Savant

So, guess what I do? I change my leaders' and teams' focus. I say to them, let's work on your strengths and talents. You have them for a reason. And it's a lot more fun – and much better for your confidence, brain, and leadership abilities. We are going to explore the brain stuff later, stay tuned …

Whether it's your own personal performance, or the performance of your team, you've probably been focused on identifying and over-coming faults, weaknesses, and shortcomings as a way to improve results. While it's certainly true that everyone is just human and has flaws and imperfections, research shows that the path to becoming great lies not in focusing on our faults, but on our strengths.

Share your strengths, not your weaknesses.

— Yogi Bhajan

In today's world, it is more important than ever that we take steps to set ourselves apart from our competition. One clear way to gain a competitive edge is to become great or exceptional in your field.

Why the 10,000 Hour Rule Supports Developing Our Strengths

Are you familiar with the work of Malcolm Gladwell? He is a best-selling author who is famous for his research in the fields of leadership, excellence, and social psychology. According to Gladwell, success in any field is based on an individual developing one or two stand-out abilities or natural talents to the point that they are no longer just competent or average, but are great.

In his 2008 book *Outliers: The Story of Success*, Gladwell popularised the concept that it takes over 10,000 hours of practice to become an expert, or great, in any field. Gladwell bases the 10,000-hour rule on research conducted by Swedish psychologist K. Anders

Ericsson, who found that it takes enormous amounts of time for anyone to move from the level of competence to greatness.

Since we only have a limited amount of lifetime, it makes sense to focus on developing our natural talents and abilities to master an area of greatness that separates us from our competition, rather than wasting time developing areas where we have little patience or natural ability. We should use the gifts we have and polish them to perfection. Guess what? YOLO – you only live once – so stop focusing on the stuff that doesn't matter.

Why Developing Strengths Gets Results

You know that you do your best work when you are doing things that come naturally to you; things that you genuinely enjoy. That's what happens when we focus on our areas of strength. We automatically improve our performance because we naturally put forth our best effort.

Wise leaders assign roles and tasks to people who have the best natural ability in those areas, making it easier for everyone to excel. As we continue to focus on our strengths, an increase in confidence, engagement, satisfaction, and performance naturally follows, and we each find happiness because we know we are doing great work.

This happiness and self-satisfaction is contagious, and it spreads to co-workers and on to your customers. Productivity improves, costs related to inefficiency decrease and our profits increase. As we begin to focus on our strengths in our personal lives, we stop wasting time on meaningless tasks and focus on fulfilling our dreams. I am going to explore some brain stuff in this book – and an area called the reticular activating system – and this will give you some insight into the power of focus and stress. In turn, when we focus on strengths, our stress levels naturally decrease and we find a natural increase of harmony and balance in our key relationships. What a great way to build happy and enthusiastic teams!

How to Identify Your Strengths

Start with you. I know that in the hustle and bustle of our daily lives it can be easy to lose sight of our strengths. Here are a couple of ways to rediscover them:

- Try to remember what past activities have brought you the most joy and satisfaction in your life. What about the activity did you enjoy most and least? What brings you happiness?

- You can gain insight into your strengths by asking close friends and relatives to name five or so qualities that describe you or five areas and natural talents that you possess.

- There are even free tests that can help you to discover your hidden strengths and abilities; you just need to search for them online. Workuno, the University of Kent, and *Psychology Today* offer three of the most well-known free online tests to help users identify their strengths, but there are countless other resources that can help you to find your key natural strengths.

- If you are still unsure of your strengths, there is a great book with an assessment that will help you find them. It is one of my favourite tools and is called *Strengths Finder 2.0* by Tom Rath – go out and buy it.

Once you've identified your strengths, seek ways to put more of your time and energy into using and developing these areas in your daily life. Even little things add up over time and the more that you can begin to play to your strengths, the happier and more energised you will become.

And guess what? You don't have to be great at everything. This is why it is important to focus on what you're good at. Therefore, surround yourself with people who have strengths and talents in other areas. Funnily enough, Richard Branson – who is an amazing leader and founder of the Virgin Group, which consists of 400 companies – isn't that great at maths. Yes, he sucks at it. There was a time when he didn't understand the difference between a net and a gross profit. Don't worry, he does now. I know how he feels. However, this weakness meant that he didn't get caught up in the detail and he could focus on the big picture. Other people can do the maths.

And look at Tim Ferriss, author of *The 4-Hour Workweek.* Did you know that his book was rejected by 25 publishers? Imagine what that might do to your confidence! Most people would give up, but Tim had a source of strength to call on, and that's what he did.

Tim realised that one thing he had going for him was his determination to step outside his comfort zone. Giving up would have been taking the easy way out, so he put his faith in himself and kept pushing, and knocking on doors. No, it wasn't an easy thing to do, but it paid off. The 26th publisher signed him up on the spot. And guess what? It wasn't the book that sealed the deal; it was Tim's strength and persistence that won over the publisher.

In *The 4-Hour Workweek,* Tim writes:

"It is far more lucrative and fun to leverage your strengths instead of attempting to fix all the chinks in your armour. The choice is between multiplication of results using strengths or incremental improvement fixing weaknesses that will, at best, become mediocre. Focus on better use of your best weapons instead of constant repair."

And those words make sense. The return on investment (ROI) on improving your strengths is far greater than it is on overcoming your weaknesses.

No one is perfect. And if you have some areas of weakness or 'areas for development' that you truly want to work on – or that are overshadowing your strengths – then go for it. Just don't focus on them. We have strengths and talents for a reason.

In turn, whether it's something in your personal or professional life, if you have tasks that you hate that are not in your area of expertise, seek ways to delegate those tasks to others who have a natural strength in those areas. This way you will have more time and energy to focus on areas in which you excel. As you continue to play to your strengths you and everyone around you will become happier and more productive.

Your strengths will also help you build your leadership brand – bring it on!

GREAT TIPS ✔

- **What are your strengths?**
  Come on, write them down!

- **I invite you to focus your mindset on them.**
  Why? We will explore this further in Chapter 7, as you are the director of your brain.

- **How would it feel to know and capitalise on your strengths?**
  Strengths make a difference. We have them for a reason.

- **Empower others by knowing their strengths.**
  Part of your role as a leader is to have this ripple effect on others. Ask those around you what their strengths are?

Focus on YOUR STRENGTHS

Chapter 6

Do You Know Your *Brand*?

This question is not trivial. *You* are a brand! Yes, you are ...

My brand is very important to me. I align my values, uniqueness, and actions based on my brand. I also have a distinct brand when it comes to what I wear, how I speak, how I write, and how I communicate. I am consistent with this brand, so when people meet me for the first time they expect me in red! My values, attitude, actions, communication and style all make up my brand.

You need to see yourself as a *brand*!

In turn, a leadership brand shows what makes you unique as a leader; what makes you different. That's what makes you special and of value to your organisation and your team. If you get your branding right you will win

Your Brand is what other people say about you when you're not in the room.

– Jeff Bezos,
CEO & founder Amazon

the positions you hope for, but if it's wrong, you just won't fit the mould.

The concept of having a personal brand is not a new one. Your brand is what separates you from others; it's your look, your reputation, and in the case of a business or product, includes a logo or sound. So your personal brand is the difference between you and anyone else.

When it comes to leadership, you *do* need to stand out in the crowd. That's really the whole point – not for ego or personal profile though, but to be seen to lead and set an example.

Your personal leadership brand says who you are.

As a leader, it's your own personal leadership branding which lets people know who you are, what you stand for, and how you work.

Identifying and strengthening your leadership brand not only communicates who you are and how you lead but also gives you focus and direction. When you're uncomfortable with a decision or strategy and it just doesn't feel right, it's probably not in alignment with who you are, what you are known for, and where you want your team to head.

One of the keys to leadership is authenticity, which gives you a foundation of strength and truth to work from, and from there you can build your leadership brand; others will look to you for leadership consistent with the strengths that you embody and display.

How to Define Your Personal Leadership Brand

When it comes to moving forward and creating anything, it is essential to understand where you start. Begin by analysing your skills and beliefs around leadership and how you see yourself.

Remember your values – they are important and are the basis of your brand. In turn, your strengths, purpose, philosophy, and presence also make up your brand! They will also make up your leadership style.

Also consider which strengths most inspire you and that you are proudest of, as these will probably be your strongest and the most admirable to those around you.

It can also be helpful in the process to consult with trusted team members or mentors to ask for feedback on how they see your leadership style and branding. It might open your eyes to perspectives you hadn't considered, as well as give you inspiration and confirmation that you are on the right track.

The key is to play to your own strengths and values, not someone else's. If the brand is not authentic and real, then it's not by definition 'personal' – and the people you lead and other stakeholders will see right through you.

Moving forward, your leadership brand needs to evolve and develop as your skills and experiences increase and improve. No personal brand is ever set in stone, any more than someone's personality and abilities.

As you change and grow as a leader, so should your personal brand.

There's no doubt that developing your leadership brand can be challenging on many levels, both personally and professionally, but that is all part of the journey and it gives us the drive to keep learning and leading. That's how you rock the role of leader.

What does your brand say about you? How would you define your brand?

Interesting questions aren't they?

Let's focus on how we can put these into action below.

GREAT TIPS ✔

- **Think about what you want to achieve.**
  Write this down.

- **Next, what do you want to be known for?**
  Again write these down and ask people around you what they think. Remember your strengths and values. Ask for feedback!

- **Define your leadership identity.**
  Look at your findings. Do the words mean something to you? Do they feel right? Do they give you something that sounds like you and something to aim for?

- **Pull it all together into a leadership brand statement.**
  This is where you work on your 'why'. Take another look at the words describing your identity. Why do they matter to you? What will you achieve through them? Try to pin it down into a sentence by using a formula like this:

  "I want to _____ so that _____."

  You might say something like, "I want to be known for honest, authentic leadership so that I can build a team that has complete confidence and trust in me."

- **Make your brand identity real.**
  Remember the chapter on 'You *Rock*' and authentic leadership? Once you determine your leadership brand and what you stand for, lead by example with authenticity.

YOU are a BRAND

Chapter 7

Brain Stuff

When I first started my company, I was working mainly in the construction and engineering space. I would walk onto these project sites with my hard hat and steel cap boots and say to these emerging leaders, "I am here to teach you leadership and emotional intelligence." Most of them (not all, thank goodness) would run for the hills. Hmm … So I decided to take a different track. I started studying neuroscience and I knew this was how I could reach these leaders. It not only made a difference to them but ultimately to me. I love this space.

What does neuroscience mean? I suppose it does sound a little technical but it is not. It is basically the brain function. The Google definition is:

"Any or all of the sciences, such as neurochemistry and experimental

It is important to remember that everyone's brain is different and life circumstances are unique to each person. However, learning about one's brain and improving the way it functions not only is vital but it is also personal.

– *Leadership is Upside Down* by Silvia Damiano

psychology, which deal with the structure or function of the nervous system and brain."

The Brain's Structure

The human brain is a remarkable organ: 73 per cent of your brain is water, and it weighs about 1.3 kilograms but uses up a massive 20 per cent of the body's energy and oxygen.

It has three main sections: the cerebrum, the cerebellum, and the brain stem. Each section of the brain is responsible for controlling a different part of the human system.

Let's take a quick look at it.

The **cerebellum** is located at the back of your brain. It's responsible for important things like managing your motor control, balance, and coordination.

The **brain stem** connects the brain to the spinal cord and it plays a key role in transmitting messages around the body. It controls functions such as breathing, heart rate, and consciousness.

The **cerebrum** is the largest part of your brain and is located at the front. It's covered by the **cerebral cortex** (your grey matter) which is divided into two hemispheres (left brain, right brain). The cerebral cortex has four lobes – the **frontal lobe, the parietal lobe, the temporal lobe, and the occipital lobe**. This section controls things like language, thought, memory, planning, and imagination.

The **prefrontal cortex** is the front section of the cerebral cortex, and is involved with things like decision making, personality, and social behaviour. It plays a vital role in recognising right from wrong and assessing consequences. It's such an active part of the brain that it uses up a lot of the body's energy.

The **limbic system** is a layer lying just under the cerebrum and it deals with memories and emotions. It is made up of different sections, including the **hypothalamus**, which produces hormones, and the **amygdalae,** which prepare the body for fight or flight. This section of the brain is very energy efficient, kicking into action only when needed.

The prefrontal cortex and the limbic system communicate closely together. The prefrontal cortex transmits social signals, and identifies whether situations are safe or threatening. The amygdalae in the limbic system react to the information, producing signals that put the body on alert. That's how we decide whether to seek safety or stand our ground.

As you can see, the brain is a very sophisticated system. You might think we've come a long way since the Stone Age, but our brains have not really evolved much at all. It's probably capable of much more than we even suspect!

One of the most exciting things about the brain is the way it can rewire itself. Called **neuroplasticity,** the brain can reorganise itself and build new pathways to meet new demands. This is really important when we try to learn a new skill or change the way we think.

The more often we practise the new behaviour, the more the brain works on building the pathways. They get stronger and stronger, eventually taking over from the old pathway altogether. This is what happens when you build new habits, and it means that we can reshape our brains whenever we need to.

And all of this goes on without us even realising it. It happens in our subconscious.

If you've ever watched mountain bike racing, you've probably wondered just how the cyclists manage to ride their bikes through the rugged terrain of the forest at such breakneck speeds without hitting a tree or other obstacle. For most of us, the sudden appearance of a large obstacle in our path causes a surge of adrenaline as our conscious minds make us aware of the danger ahead. Listening to our conscious mind, we might simply freeze!

Yet these cyclists seem to magically fly by these obstacles without slowing down, completely unscathed, and with only a slight change in their course. How do they do it? The answer lies in the cyclist's ability to allow their subconscious to direct their mind and remain focused on their goal.

The Power of the Mind

The secret lies in the power of the mind. The cyclists have, through practice and experience, learnt to trust the intuition of their inner voice and allow their subconscious the freedom to direct their course.

Of course, the power of our mind is not limited to safely guiding us when we are riding a bicycle. Your mind can help you to achieve more happiness and success in life if you will learn to trust your inner voice and allow your subconscious the freedom to direct your course in your daily life.

Becoming the Director of Your Mind

Here is why this matters. Once I had a coaching session with an amazing emerging leader; it was booked for 8am in the city and she was late. She was lost. She was calling me and freaking out. I told her to take a deep breath and gave her further instructions on how to get to where I was located. When she finally arrived (only 14 minutes late) she was flustered, upset, and concerned about first impressions.

First impressions! I don't do first impressions, as I have been proven wrong too many times. I could tell immediately she wasn't in the right frame of mind. Instead of walking into my office, I took her to the park and we sat in a deck chair. I told her to close her eyes and follow my voice, breathe deeply and focus on this. After a few minutes of mindfulness, relaxation, and a refocus, she was a different person. I asked her how she felt, and she replied, "Amazing." I told her she just needed to get her mind back on track as she is her own director.

You are the director of your brain. *You* are in control of your mind. Think about this. Your mind is like a stage. You are the director of this stage. What actors are playing out on this stage? You only want Oscar award winning actors on this stage. If you have bad actors on the stage (your mind) you will have a pretty crappy play and no one will want to buy tickets.

This matters in leadership. Our brain is our most important leadership tool. The more you get the power of the mind, your mind, the more effective you will be.

- **Be specific.** In order to get your mind to work for you, it is important that you learn to think in specific terms when it comes to your goals. Make time to be alone with your thoughts each day and really focus on the specifics of what you want to achieve. Think about those things that bring you joy and work to include more of these activities into your daily life. Doing so will help to bring positive energy into your life and help you to feel calmer and more centred.

- **Focus.** We get what we focus on. Think about this. How often have you woken up and thought to yourself, this is going to be a bad day, and everything that happens is *bad*! You can change your focus. This is why I set my mind up every day to focus on the positive, so I can see it. You have the power to choose your own focus, so use it wisely.

- **Do one thing.** Choose one thing to work on and do it well. Splitting your focus and concentration across a number of tasks or problems only means that none of them have the attention they deserve. What is important to you right now? That's what you need to work on.

- **Know your attention spans and cycles.** Perhaps you're a morning person. Perhaps you can work for three or four hours straight before you need a break. Or perhaps you're someone who can't get started until you've had a couple of coffees and a chat. It makes sense to work when your brain is ready, doesn't it? We're all different and we have different peak times for working and taking a break. Pay attention to how you feel throughout the day and take a break when you need it. You won't do your best work when you're tired and your mind begins to wander.

- **Be mindful.** Notice what you are doing and thinking. When things are going along as expected, the brain switches to autopilot and all those familiar thoughts pop up from the default network in the brain. This is the path where your thoughts always go, whether you are aware of it or not. For example, you're driving home when you suddenly realise that you haven't noticed the last few kilometres you've driven – but somehow you've planned out the night's menu. When your brain operates this way, you are missing out on all sorts of experiences and information that you could take in and use, particularly through your senses. Being mindful means living in and experiencing the moment, and it's a skill you will need to practise if you really want to direct your own mind.

As you think about what you want to achieve each day, be mindful of the types of thoughts that try to enter your mind. Learn to control negative thoughts, worries, and doubts and replace your negative thoughts and self-doubts with positive affirmations and self-talk that builds your self-esteem.

Here are a few examples of popular positive affirmations:

- I know, accept, and trust myself.
- I make the right choices every time.
- I forgive myself for my mistakes and learn from them.
- I know I can accomplish anything I set my mind to.
- I forgive myself and set myself free.

- I never give up.

- I accept what I cannot change.

- I release the past and live fully in the present moment.

Ways to make changes happen

In one exercise I use with my clients I ask them to imagine they are standing behind themselves by a couple of metres. I then tell them to just look at themselves, asking with a curious mindset, "What's happening with that person right now? What's going on? I wonder what that person is thinking." Taking that step back clears your mind more than you realise is possible.

As you learn to be specific in your goals, and direct your thoughts to be more positive than negative, you will find that your thoughts are less scattered and more focused. You will start to achieve greater success in reaching your goals. Rather than focusing on the obstacles that block you from achieving your goals, your mind will automatically look for ways to help you create situations in your life that help you to reach your goals. Over time, you will learn how to hear the inner voice of your subconscious, you will begin to trust it to direct your course, and you will become the director of your mind.

Remember – to be a successful leader you often have to create a strong foundation with the bricks others throw at you. It starts with you. That foundation is with you.

RAS Setting

If you want to change your art, change your habits.

— Clement Greenberg

Have you ever looked at buying a car, then made a decision on what you want, and suddenly start seeing that car everywhere? Everyone is driving a BMW convertible! Not that I really want that car ... but now that I have just written this, I am seeing BMW convertibles everywhere! I want one! In *red*!

That was your reticular activating system (RAS) in action. Your RAS is the automatic trigger in your brain that allows you to hone in on important and relevant information ... even when you think you're not paying attention.

Your RAS is essentially a self-programmed filter between your conscious and subconscious minds. You place those filters in your mind. You don't even have to think about it. For instance, no one needs to tell you to listen for your child's voice. It's inherent. It's programmed in.

So watch what you focus on! If you want to focus on your weaknesses, they are what you will see. Oh wait, there is a weakness. Yeah, there is another one. And think what that will do to your self-esteem and confidence! You are the director of your brain – so focus your RAS on your strengths, talents, and the positives!

Focus on what makes you rock! It will change your life and leadership.

GREAT TIPS ✔

- **Observe your thoughts.**
  Be present and observe your thoughts. Even if it is just for 10 minutes. You can't work on a problem you don't know about. Once you observe your thinking, you will know where to start. Remember the RAS too – attention goes, energy flows.

- **Choose a positive affirmation each and every day.**
  In the morning, decide on an affirmation. You'll repeat it silently to yourself as you go about your day. Maybe it's something as simple as "I will never give up" or "I'm an amazing leader." Using an affirmation will not only give you something positive to think about, but it also takes up time your brain might otherwise use for negative thoughts.

- **Make a gratitude list.**
  Every day write and reflect on your successes and the positives for the day. Remember you are the director of your brain. Making a gratitude list can alter your mood and keep you focused on the positive in life.

You are the
DIRECTOR
OF YOUR BRAIN

Chapter 8

Squash the ANTs

I am not talking about those ants that crawl onto your blanket at a Sunday family picnic. I am talking about those ANTs that crawl into your brain. Now I am a glass half-full type of leader – but I do on occasion (we all do) have ANTs!

Do you have ANTs running freely in your mind? ANTs, or automatic negative thoughts, are dangerous creatures. ANTs are those negative thoughts that always seem to be in the back of your mind, regardless of the situation. ANTs make it impossible to relax and enjoy the moment, because they manage to sniff out the negative aspect of any event.

Negative thoughts rob you of being able to feel joy or happiness in the present. When you are unable to control your thoughts, negative thoughts end up leaving you feeling worried, cynical,

Your time is limited; so don't waste it living someone else's life. Don't be trapped by dogma – which is living with the results of other people's thinking. Don't let the noise of other's opinions drown out your own voice.

– Steve Jobs

frustrated, drained, depressed, and defeated. Over time, negative thoughts can have a dreadful impact on your physical and mental wellbeing, and your ability to achieve your life goals.

Believe me, with all the thousands of thoughts going on in our mind, we have a lot of negative ones. Sometimes I let these ANTs invade my brain. Sounds pretty disgusting, doesn't it? This is when things like resilience and mindfulness can be really powerful. I squash these ANTs.

I step back and say to myself, "Is this thought empowering or disempowering?" We all get them. *I am not good, enough. I am not pretty enough, smart enough, skinny enough,* blah, blah, blah. I squash them! *Big time!* You know what? I am not the smartest, prettiest, or skinniest but I am good enough. I am good enough just the way I am. I am not perfect and it's my imperfections that make me great.

If your thoughts are not empowering, squash them. Also, as much as I am an advocate for listening to people's views and feedback about me as a leader, I don't take it all on board. This can be hard. Remember, people are telling you what they think through their lens or perspective. Believe me, in my career and since starting a company, I have had many people tell me their views and opinions about me and my work. Some of it was empowering and some not. It is much easier for the brain to listen to and take on board a 'feedback sandwich' and focus on the negative in the middle.

It doesn't mean it is true. I also ask myself if the person who is telling me this is someone I trust and respect. Only take on board what truly matters to you, what you feel can you learn from and build on, and what will ultimately empower you. Let the rest of it go. It doesn't matter.

The good news is that despite how destructive automatic negative thoughts can be, most of us can learn how to regain control of our mind and retrain our brains to overcome the power of negative thoughts.

How ANTs Form

According to the Centre for Redeployment Psychology, all of our thoughts – whether they are our memories of actual events that happened, or simply random musings and dreams – come to mind as the result of nerve impulses. Usually there is some sort of internal or external event, such as a person, place, or thing that triggers the firing of a nerve impulse to make your mind aware of the thought. The nerve impulses generated by both positive and negative thoughts travel along the same pathways in our brain. These pathways are flexible, so they can be shaped and controlled, and over time we can literally reprogram our brains.

Current research shows that no matter how painful or negative some of our past memories might be, we can each learn to become aware of negative thoughts as they occur, and choose to replace these thoughts with more positive ones. Over time, as we actively practise substituting positive thoughts for negative ones, we can break the power that negative thoughts and memories have over our lives, and move towards a more positive and healthy frame of mind.

Steps to Take to Squash Your ANTs

1. **Look for positives**. To begin to conquer your ANTs, you will first need to identify some positive thoughts to have ready

so that you can substitute and focus on them, rather than the negative thoughts.

2. **Identify your triggers**. Once you have several positive thoughts to use in place of the negative thoughts, learn to identify the triggers of your negative thoughts. Are there certain events, places, or people that seem to increase the likelihood of their occurrence? Learn to remain calm when you come in contact with one of these triggers.

3. **Learn to relax**. Learning relaxation techniques such as mindfulness and meditation, and focusing on your breathing, can help you remain calm when you encounter a trigger for your ANTs. As you become aware of a negative thought, remain calm, focus on your breathing or other relaxation technique, and then consciously substitute the positive thought in its place.

4. **Preparing for the trigger**. Let's use an example. Do you often feel nervous before you have to give a speech? Does your mind become filled and eventually overwhelmed with images of the mistakes you just know you will make? By the time you actually give your speech, the ANTs have full control. Your negative thoughts become a self-fulfilling prophecy and you make the same mistakes that you obsessed over. You know what I do? I spend about 10 minutes prior to a speaking gig or presentation stepping on ANTs and using positive affirmations. I also think about times I truly rocked it – as well as my power poses (more on that later in this book!). Let's explore this a little more.

In a situation like this, it is important to realise beforehand that you feel anxious in such a setting. Before the day of your speech, practise remaining calm, focusing on your breathing, and then substituting your positive image in place of the ANTs. In this case, you might imagine yourself being calm and remaining in control during your speech, and your audience actively listening to what you have to say and enjoying the event. At the conclusion of your speech, the crowd heartily applauds your performance.

Practise this positive thought each day as you lead up to your speech and start each day off right with positive affirmations that help to boost your self-esteem. When the time comes, focus on remaining calm and visualising your positive thoughts and you will find that your mind is so powerful it will work to make your positive vision come true!

You can apply this same technique to virtually any negative thought or memory that can come to your mind. By identifying your negative thoughts and memories, actively watching for them, and substituting a positive thought in their place, you will unleash the power of your mind and it will squash your ANTs for you. Over time, you will overcome more obstacles, reach more goals, and improve your sense of self-worth, wellbeing, and even your overall health! And finally your confidence! Confidence is so hot right now …

What are your ANTs? How can you *squash* them?

P.S. They are just ANTs and they do *not* have power over you.

GREAT TIPS ✔

- **Take up mindfulness or meditation.**
  There is more and more evidence of the power of mindfulness and meditation on the brain. Find some great resources, tools, and books to help you.

- **Know your triggers.**
  The more you know about yourself, the more you will be prepared and know how to deal with them. I used to have a thing around failing. I hated it with a passion. Of course, no one likes to fail. I knew this trigger and worked on changing my thinking around it. I reframed it and thought if I do fail, what can I learn from it?

- **Smile.**
  It really does help your negative thinking and stress. I laugh at myself all the time.

- **Surround yourself with positive people (I call them my tribe).**
  Please surround yourself with people who also have positive thoughts. They will in turn empower you to be the best you can be. Get rid of anyone who is glass half-empty; they will only bring you and your thoughts down (if you let them!).

What we think,

WE BECOME

The Buddha

Chapter 9

Confidence is *Hot*

Other students used to call me "Sonia Sonia study head, all she does is study" at school. At the time, I do remember wondering why they all said that. Doesn't everyone study hard, and what is wrong with working hard? Well, nothing. But why did I study *so* hard? I really do believe it was because I wanted to build confidence, self-belief, and feel better about myself. Somehow I knew that being really competent would make me feel confident. There is nothing wrong with that. But I didn't put my hand up for so many things, because I didn't feel truly competent and hence confident.

I truly believe confidence matters just as much (or maybe a little more) than competence. Yes, it *does!*

Why do we need to be competent at something before we feel confident?

The most beautiful thing you can wear is confidence.

– Blake Lively

Confidence is *hot*. Think about it: you could be really competent at something and if you don't have confidence, it doesn't matter. You'll probably never do it! Confidence rocks.

We all know confident leaders. They light up a room when they arrive and they always leave a positive impression. They seem to have an indefinable something that makes them special, and perhaps even inspiring.

Very little stands in the way of emulating the confidence of those leaders who inspire you. And it's unlikely they were born so confident. It took mindfulness and practice, so if they can do it so can you.

These are just some of the behaviours of a confident leader.

They use their words wisely, with respect and consideration.
This is particularly true when speaking of others. They have no need to gossip, or drag others down to make themselves feel better. Leaders with confidence are too excited by their plans and dreams.

They don't take anything personally.
Leaders who lead confidently know the only person they can control is themselves, and they are not responsible for anyone else's emotions or behaviours. You cannot control what others do, only how you react.

They use their power for good.
They know their strengths and capabilities, and seek opportunities to make the world around them just a little better. Whether that's by mentoring someone in their team and helping them achieve

their own goals, or fighting for human rights, they are selfless and share their talent with others.

They give credit where credit is due.
Confident leaders won't take credit for another's success. Firstly, they have more respect for themselves and others, but also they celebrate the achievements of others, and the satisfaction of having assisted on the journey is more than enough. They support each other, and don't compete with them. Do not compete!

They trust their instincts.
They are thorough and decisive, and when they have made a decision they stick to it. They don't hesitate or second-guess, and this in turn instils confidence and motivates the team they lead.

They don't lead to be liked.
Confident leaders are not afraid to make the tough decisions even though they may not be popular. They can handle opposition and will deal with it rationally and fairly, with the conviction to stand by any decision. Those they lead respect them for their ability to follow through and be consistent.

They learn from their mistakes.
Bumps in the road do not knock confident leaders off course. They do not expect perfection from themselves or others, and know that with success and responsibility comes risk and sometimes failure. The ability to get up and get on with it after a setback keeps them moving forward, and inspires others.

They believe in balance and reward.
Working hard in the times of heavy workload is balanced with a break and reward for the team when the job is done and the load

lightens a little. Confident leaders lead by example and put in the big hours when required, but they are not afraid to celebrate and regroup and take a breather in preparation for the next challenge ahead.

They don't waste time on worry.
What-ifs and should-have-beens don't exist for the leader who is confident in their leadership. Worry changes nothing and is a waste of energy and focus that can be better used to move forward.

They are authentic.
Remember our chapter, You *Rock*? Understanding their own motivations and being clear about their beliefs ensures that confident leaders inspire and motivate effectively, credibly and consistently. Insincerity is obvious and unacceptable to those you lead, even if they can't quite identify what's not right. Authenticity is central to leaders with confidence.

They are not perfect.
Striving for perfection is a confidence killer! Instead, accept imperfection; yes, you heard me. Miss deadlines (we all can do this), get lost, forget to reply to emails, miss meetings, and show up to something late. It is going to be okay, trust me.

> *The essence of being human is that one does not seek perfection.*
> — George Orwell

By the way, I tried being perfect and it doesn't work. Bring on imperfection and do something radical for a change – be yourself!

Finally – and this is important – confident leaders do not compare themselves with others!

Theodore Roosevelt once said, "Comparison is the thief of joy." Listen to this one.

So as a leader, if you show you are unsure of yourself, people won't listen, and if you don't believe in the course you set, others won't be motivated and inspired to follow you.

Guess what? You've got this. You are a confident leader. Confidence is a choice. And action breeds courage and confidence.

What will it take for you to be confident?

GREAT TIPS ✔

- **Fail fast and move forward.**
  The more things you try, the more often you will fail, and that's okay. You learn much more from failure than you do from success. Read more about this in Chapter 15.

- **Don't compare.**
  What you see isn't always real. People can appear to be or achieve so much more than they really do. Comparing is a confidence killer!

- **Stand straight.**
  Ban the slouch! You might not believe it, but when you stand up straight it can make you feel more confident. We will explore this more in Chapter 12.

- **Carefully pick the people you hang out with.**
  These are the people you see all the time and you'll pick up attitudes and beliefs from them. So choose people who have the right kind of approach to life – positive and willing to give things a go.

- **Dress the part!**
  This doesn't mean blowing your budget! Expensive clothes aren't necessary, believe me; I am an eBay buyer! Choose clothes that make you feel successful – well-fitting and stylish. Finally, don't be afraid of some colour; black is professional, but I have to say it is colour that gets noticed. For example, I wear a lot of floral and red – and it always gets noticed.

- **Learn. Keep learning.**
  You can never know too much! The people you admire are probably trying to learn something new each day. The best leaders are the ones who keep learning. Read Chapter 21 if you want to know more.

- **Be kind to yourself.**
  When those ANTs pop into your head – squash them. I had to remind you of this from the last chapter. Would you speak to a friend like this? No. Don't speak to yourself in a negative way.

- **Believe in yourself.**
  You are capable of so much more than you really know, and you won't find out how much until you start trusting in yourself. You are clever, intuitive, and caring. We know it. It's time you did, too.

Be
AUTHENTIC!

Be
RADICAL!

Be
YOURSELF!

Chapter 10

Courage

We have talked about confidence as I think this is pivotal. But, leadership is also about courage. It took real courage for me to start my own business and I will talk about it later in Chapter 25, *Jumping Off the Cliff*. It is the key to great leadership. Leadership takes courage. Lead with courage.

It occurs to me every day how much courage the leaders that I am coaching and working with have.

Aristotle called courage the first virtue, because it makes all of the other virtues possible. Courage means "The ability to do something that frightens. Bravery and strength in the face of pain or grief."

My days have been filled with courage, bravery, and strength. I have had years of meeting leaders who

> I learned that courage was not the absence of fear, but the triumph over it. The brave man is not he who does not feel afraid, but he who conquers that fear.
>
> — Nelson Mandela

have been made redundant, years of coaching leaders who don't think they are good enough, years of leaders being told they are not performing, years of leaders trying to get that dream job but not succeeding. Years of leaders trying to build businesses and their dreams asking for help, and years of leaders who are putting themselves out there to be the best they can be after I had coached and inspired them to go for it. Years of leaders also being truly vulnerable.

Thing is, I work with – and live and breathe – courage every day.

Showing up and being authentically who you are is courage; fighting for what you believe in is courage; putting your hand up is courage; asking for help is courage; starting your own business is courage; letting people go who don't serve you is courage; getting back up when you are knocked down is courage; and being the best leader you can be is courage. We are courageous every day of our lives.

Often I work with leaders trying to be someone else, lacking the bravery and courage to go for what they want and letting others bring them down. Yet I know it's in them, deep down, some-where …

Be who *you* are, own it, and focus on what makes you rock! We are all different. Focus your mind and thoughts on what makes you different, brilliant, and unique. You will start to see and feel the difference created from focusing your mind on your strengths, talents, and how *you* make a difference to others and this world.

No one is perfect. Remember this. Life is about putting yourself out there. Life is about learning and growing. There are plenty of things I am not great at. And if I want to be better at something or be the best I can be, I read, work with a coach and mentors, attend conferences, and connect with people who can help – I open my mind to learning and change. I love being different. I love learning.

Go for it. If I can do it, you can. If you really want that role, to work with that company, meet that person (I found a great mentor on LinkedIn, asked to meet him, and asked him to be my mentor – he said yes!), to start a business, follow a dream, visit that place, or whatever that goal might be – go for it. Do it. I started my company from a *blog!* Why? Because I believed in myself and loved leadership. And I thought to myself, worst-case scenario is that I gave it a go and it didn't work out. Sure I was scared but I lived beyond the fear and jumped.

Courage is being scared to death ... and saddling up anyway.
— John Wayne

Do you know the story of Nancy Wake? She was also known as the White Mouse during World War II.

Born in New Zealand, Nancy grew up in Australia, training as a nurse. In 1932 she moved to England and then travelled to Europe where she trained as a journalist. Early in her career she interviewed Hitler, so she was very aware of what was beginning to happen around her.

In 1939 she married a wealthy Frenchman, but then war broke out. She and her husband joined the new French Resistance, helping Allied servicemen and Jewish refugees to flee the country.

She was fortunate to be married to a wealthy man because it gave Nancy access to areas other people couldn't reach. She and her husband bought an ambulance which she used to help people escape. Her nursing skills came in handy at these times.

By 1942 the Nazis were aware that there was someone causing them problems, although they didn't know it was Nancy Wake. They called her the White Mouse and soon she topped their most wanted list.

Nancy and her husband had to flee France, too. After a short period of imprisonment, she finally escaped to England where she resumed her resistance work. As if that wasn't brave enough, knowing what was ahead of her, Nancy parachuted back into France in 1944 to help with the D-Day landings.

She led a team of 7,000 Maquis troops who fought guerrilla-style to keep the Nazis occupied and give the best chance to the Allies as they landed. Without Nancy Wake's brave leadership, the war might very well have ended differently.

She was strong; she was stubborn; she was willing to get her hands dirty; and she wouldn't ask her troops to do anything she didn't do.

However, it is her **courage** she is remembered for, and that was the key to her powerful leadership. She did things no woman of her time and status should have been doing. But she had a vision, and she had the courage to see it through.

You can imagine that many of her ideas weren't popular with everyone, but when she believed she was right, there was little that could stop her. She stood her ground and explained her reasons, and inspired others to follow.

Courageous leaders are honest and tenacious. They stand out because they will fight for what they believe in.

War-time leadership is tough and dangerous, but Nancy Wake, despite her nickname, was as strong and passionate as a lion. She was daring and she was unstoppable. How inspiring would that be to people who are looking for direction and a solution?

It's obviously not so dramatic in the workplace, but great leaders still need to have the same qualities – **honesty, authenticity, vision, bravery, and dedication.**

These are the qualities that capture the hearts and minds of your teams and make people want to follow you. This is where the leader stands out against the managers. Leaders don't have to tell you what to do. They inspire you to *want* to do it.

Courage is not the absence of fear; it's the willingness to take action because you are being powered by a strong belief that what you are doing is the right thing.

You don't have to be a Nancy Wake, but if you adopt her approach to leadership, you will find that the boundaries you used to accept are suddenly shattered. You and your team will achieve things you have only dreamed of.

Only those who will risk going too far can possibly find out how far one can go.

— T.S. Eliot

Be courageous and be defined by you. Do not let others define you. Over the years I have had my critics, and I have also had my brilliant supporters. I have had amazing guidance and feedback as well as negative and downright unnecessary comments. I don't define myself by them, and only listen to those who truly matter. I always follow my heart and intuition. There is great courage in doing so.

Leadership is about courage. It is truly brave to be who you truly are. Step up and lead. Believe and trust yourself. Only you matter. You are worthy.

This is courage.

What does courage mean to you? What courageous action can you do today?

GREAT TIPS ✔

- **Courage means being afraid and acting anyway.**
  Just do it.

- **Courage is a habit.**
  Most of us aren't born courageous, so we shouldn't expect to magically acquire it without practice. As Brené Brown writes in her book *The Gifts of Imperfection*, "Courage is … a habit, a virtue: You get it by courageous acts. It's like you learn to swim by swimming. You learn courage by couraging."

- **Learn to attend to positive signals in your courage and let go of the negative.**
  I remember when I first started public speaking; I would notice the people in the room who seemed disengaged and then I thought my speaking sucked. It stopped me putting myself out there. I decided to keep going and now I only focus on the positive people in the audience.

- **Find role models of courageous people.**
  This is important. I follow, read, and surround myself with people who have the courage to be seen, follow their dreams, take risks, and stand up for what they believe in.

- **Feel the fear and do it anyway.**
  Yes, a little cheesy but life is too short not to be courageous. Life can be scary. It is easier for the brain to gravitate towards the fear and threat – and this can stop us. You are the director of your brain, your life, and your leadership. Feel it, and do it. Be courageous every day.

LEAD *with* COURAGE

Chapter 11

Presence – How Do You Turn Up?

Presence – you know it when you are surrounded by it. Difficult to define, it is the executive presence that inspires others to become better, and the essence that all prospective business leaders seek. Have you been surrounded by someone who clearly has that special something, that presence that makes people want to listen and follow in their footsteps? History is full of great leaders, and modern business executives are no exception. Wouldn't you love to be them for just a few minutes and own the room? Wouldn't you like to command everyone's attention with confidence, grace, and humour?

Now think about a time when you have had to listen to a leader ramble on about a topic that did not draw you in or make you want to act. A little embarrassing, right? The speaker clearly had no presence to speak of in

My sign is Leo. A Leo has to walk with pride. When he takes a step, he has to put his foot down. You walk into a room and you want people to know your presence, without you doing anything.

– Wesley Snipes

this scenario. I am certain you wouldn't want to be this person, regardless of the size of their pay cheque. No, you want to be inspirational, noticeable, follow-able, and likeable.

It doesn't matter what field or industry you work in, having a strong presence is crucial to your position. The great thing about the ever-elusive presence, however, is that it can be learned. One really awesome source to teach you to do just that is a book which I highly recommend, entitled *Own the Room: Discover Your Signature Voice to Master Your Leadership Presence,* written by Amy Jen Su and Muriel Maignan Wilkins. These two executive coaches enable leaders or prospective leaders to discover their signature voice (both the inner voice and the voice of others) and develop their leadership presence.

While you may have trouble defining leadership presence yourself, Su and Wilkins define it as "the ability to consistently and clearly articulate your value proposition while influencing and connecting with others." This presence is deeply seated in authenticity, like many other modern-day approaches, and is a huge component of leadership today.

Together the authors developed a holistic approach called ACE conditioning: assumptions, communication strategies, and energy. I truly like it, and use this approach every time I walk into a meeting or speak on stage.

Let's take a closer look at the three areas.

Assumptions: The premise here is to know your assumptions and how they propel you or restrain you. Whether you realise it or not, your assumptions can affect your daily interactions, methodologies, and your work approach. Having a clear understanding of your values and your beliefs plays a big part in it. In turn, before I go on stage to speak I am conscious of my assumptions. If I am saying to myself, *I can't,* then guess what? I can't. I say to myself, *I can.*

Communication strategies: What are you trying to say? And how are you going to say it? Communication can make or break a mood so ensure that your personal style of communication is working for you. Practice makes perfect, and make sure you are proactive. I know my communication style and who is in the audience. I stay true to my 'audience self' and communicate in a way that is me and is also how I can best influence those around me.

Energy: How energetic you are can affect everything else from your language style to your mood. Even if your heart is not in it, act like it is. You need to find the physicality to back up your words and your non-verbal communication in particular, as it might just be saying something else altogether. This is why energy is important. Think about it: have you ever experienced someone walking into a room and sapping the energy out because they were in a bad mood? Please watch your energy.

So stop with those negative thoughts or assumptions that you will never achieve true leadership presence. Like most leadership skills, they can be learned. You just need to find the time and the motivation to break those patterns. If you are willing, then you will find a way. You'll rock it!

We have covered the importance of presence, and next I am going to share how your body language shapes who you are.

How are you showing up?

GREAT TIPS ✔

- **Remember to watch your assumptions, energy, and communication.**
  These areas really matter, and make a huge difference to your presence.

- **Hone your conversation skills.**
  Leaders who have presence are able to put people at ease. This can be difficult at times, but remember the more you make people feel safe, the more they will trust you. Hence you will have more presence.

- **Focus on character and authenticity.**
  It can't be stressed enough that leadership presence is an inside-out job. Always be authentic and remember your character is everything. Be true and know yourself.

- **Be present.**
  Being present is fundamental. Truly. Present. Not thinking about your emails or looking at your phone whilst talking to someone. Be there, and give them the gift of your presence.

Be truly PRESENT

Chapter 12

Stand Tall and Own It!

I really can't believe I remember this, but I was working at a restaurant while going through university and I was standing in the middle of this restaurant with my hands on my hips.

A woman came up to me (I didn't know her) and pulled my hands down off my hips and told me to stop. Why? She said it didn't look ladylike. I thought, "Are you kidding?" But I stopped. I wish I hadn't.

Did you know that your body language directly affects your life and career success? It's true.

In an experiment with soccer players, it was found that their stance had a direct bearing on how the player was perceived. Penalty takers with dominant body language were perceived more positively by soccer goalkeepers

Be sure you put your feet in the right place, then stand firm.

— Abraham Lincoln

and players and were expected to perform better than players with submissive body language.

An experiment at Harvard in 2012, outlined in *The Benefit of Power Posing Before a High-Stakes Social Evaluation*, produced similar findings. It tested whether "changing nonverbal behaviour prior to a high-stakes social evaluation could improve performance in the evaluated task." As predicted, high-power posers performed better and were more likely to be chosen for hire.

It's the same in the workplace. If you look successful, people think you *are* successful and will see you as highly credible. Just think what that might do for your career advancement.

Social psychologist Amy Cuddy, who co-wrote the Harvard paper mentioned above, has built her recent career doing research into body language and speaking and writing about how we can change other people's perceptions simply by changing body positions. More importantly, we can change our own body chemistry in the same way.

The Power Pose of Success

The use of the power pose, which is taking up a confident stance even if you don't feel confident, can raise your testosterone levels and reduce the level of the stress hormone, cortisol, in your brain.

What Is a Power Pose?

Close your eyes and picture a winner. They stand tall and straight, chin up, eyes wide open, and their arms are often opened up. They are proud of themselves and take the space to show it. That's a power pose.

Now picture the loser. Head drooping, shoulders rounded in defeat, and taking up a small physical space. That's the pose of the defeated.

Try a power pose now. I am telling you it works!

Stand up and spread your legs wide. Put your hands on your hips, take a breath, and puff your chest out. Notice how you automatically stand straighter and your head is high? Hold that position for a couple of minutes. Now pay attention to how you feel. Good, huh?

It takes less than two minutes for the changes to kick in inside your brain and to affect your confidence. So, a power pose not only reflects power, it also *creates* it inside you.

Choosing When to Use the Power Pose

The power pose is a position of dominance so it's not something to use all the time, especially when working as part of a team. Believe me I don't go up to everyone and stand like Wonder Woman or stretch my arms out to feel more confidence. I definitely do it before I speak on stage though!

The best time to use the power pose is to even up a power imbalance or to boost your confidence. For example, when you are being interviewed for a promotion, a power pose makes you look confident and convincing to the authority figures that are interviewing you. Another time to use this technique is when you are about to make a presentation and you need more confidence than you are feeling. A power pose kicks your brain into high gear.

Pay attention to the winners around you – the people who are successful within your industry – and study their body language. Spot the way they sit and stand and the way they dominate their space. They aren't just doing it for image. They are also doing it to boost their own confidence and self-belief.

Knowing that you can have control over your own body chemistry, how might you use it to boost your own chances of career success?

By the way, I teach this in *all* my programs and every single leader that puts this into practice says it *works!*

> Our bodies change our minds,
> our minds change our behaviour,
> and our behaviour changes our outcomes.

Now go out there and show them! And don't let anyone take your hands off your hips!

When could you use the power pose?

No one can make you feel inferior without your consent. – Eleanor Roosevelt

GREAT TIPS ✔

- **This is the *best* tip in this book.**
  Do the power pose.

STAND TALL.

You are a leader.

Chapter 13

Leader's Balance

I am not a fan of the term 'work-life balance' but I'm constantly asked about it. Why? I think the work-life balance thing can put pressure on us and therefore we lose the meaning of the term *balance*. I focus on doing what I love and being truly present. Let me explain.

My work is a great part of my life and I love it, so I don't see it as work. I know I am lucky. My daughter is the biggest and most amazing part of my life. My friends and family are amazing, too. My continuous learning and growth is part of my life. And doing things that I really love to do is part of my life. Thing is, they are all loves of mine. I only focus on my work and purpose, and the things that make a difference in my world. As leaders, we get caught up in the trivial things – the things

Real generosity towards the future lies in giving all to the present.

– Albert Camus

that don't matter. Don't focus on the sand and the water in the jar. Focus on the *rocks!*

There is this notion that we can have it all. We can't have it all, all at once. Sure there are lots of things I love to do, want to achieve, and places I would love to explore. They will come in time, when it is right. We can get caught up in goals, achievement, success, and lots of doing. Focus on what you love and what is important *right* now. If I got caught up in everything I want to do and achieve, my brain might explode. And it can be debilitating. I need to focus on the few things that serve me right now and put them into my energy buckets – and not let the trivial stuff creep in.

It is also important that you love what you do. I know this can be tough at times. Believe me, there are days I don't love my work – when I have a disappointed client (this is rare), an unsuccessful tender, too much travel, and I miss my family – there are those times. Then I always focus on my purpose and target my thoughts to why I do what I do, and the difference I am making. Can you do this? Try it.

Why is what you do at work important? Is it important to you to serve customers, help the community, build a team, and make a difference? See the joy and love for what you do. Being present is paramount.

Psychologist Mihaly Csikszentmihaltyi says, "Flow is being completely involved in an activity for its own sake. The ego falls away. Time flies. Every action, movement and thought follows inevitably from the previous one, like playing jazz." So be there – truly there; whether it is good, bad, ugly, or brilliant, be there. Your present circumstances don't dictate your destination.

Part of the leader's balance is *you*. Take time out for you. We all get caught up in the *busyness* of life. I am so busy; you are so busy. I always reframe this to myself and others. I say I am hard-working, not busy. It is important as a leader that you allow your team as well as yourself to have brain breaks, time out, and just do nothing occasionally. Why? Sometimes the best insights and ideas come to us when we clear our minds. You need to respect and love your mind. Give it a break. Give your team a break. Allow yourself and others to empty the mind of all thoughts and just be.

What do you love to do? Focus on your rocks.

One of my favourite authors, Shawn Achor, says that happiness is a choice. "It is a choice about where your single processor brain will devote its finite resources as you process the world. If you scan for the negative first, your brain literally has no resources left over to see the things you are grateful for or the meaning embedded in your work. But if you scan the world for the positive, you start to reap an amazing advantage."

So be mindful every day. Pay attention to what you are doing and experience every living moment. Be present and squeeze the delicious juice out of every minute.

Now, if you're asking yourself why this is important to your leadership role, let me tell you that I haven't gone all woo-woo on you.

Achor reports research showing that happiness raises nearly every business and educational outcome: raising sales by 37 per cent, productivity by 31 per cent, and accuracy on tasks by 19 per cent, as well as providing myriad health and quality-of-life improvements.

So it's not just a feel-good matter; it has a direct impact on our lives and on the bottom line business. It's really *that* important.

Where you put your energy is where you'll find your results. If you put your energies into complaining and seeing what's wrong with life, you're going to be unhappy. But if you focus on what's great about life, you hold the secret to happiness.

By being present in each moment you will discover what really makes you happy. Then you can do more of it. Pour your energies all over that good stuff and live an awesome life! Lead and be the way.

GREAT TIPS ✔

- **Get the word 'busyness' out of your language.**
  As a leader you want to be approachable. I use the word hard-working. I want my team and peers to feel like they can talk to or approach me any time.

- **Put your energy and time into things that truly matter.**
  Get rid of time wasters.

- **Write down what makes you happy and do it.**
  Focus on your rocks and things that really matter.

- **Unplug each day.**
  Technology was supposed to make things easier for us. It can if you manage it. Take time out of your day to stop and just be present; go for a walk, listen and watch your surroundings, or spend a couple of hours without your phone. The world will keep spinning. Let go of all the noise.

- **Be mindful.**
  Jon Kabat-Zinn defines mindfulness as: "The awareness that emerges through paying attention on purpose, in the present moment, and non-judgmentally to the unfolding of experience moment by moment." My favourite word here is *non-judgmental*.

FOCUS
on the
ROCKS

Chapter 14

Passion. It Matters

This might be a shock to you but I am passionate about what I do.

Why? Easy. Leadership is my why, purpose, and passion.

It matters. Truly matters.

Think of it like this. There are *a lot*, I mean *a lot*, of consultants, companies, and coaches that work in the leadership space. We all pretty much have the same purpose (well I hope so!). Now, imagine working with a company or coach who doesn't have passion for what they do versus someone who truly loves and believes in what they do – and they show it! I bet you would want to work with the person who is passionate!

Martin Luther King Jr. Richard Branson. Steve Jobs. Oprah Winfrey.

Nothing is as important as passion. No matter what you want to do with your life, be passionate.

– Jon Bon Jovi

All incredibly passionate leaders. They truly love and believe in their purpose and vision – and this is why we want more of it! People didn't follow *"I think I might have a dream."*

They followed *"I have a dream!"*

Passion is contagious. I do this passion activity all the time in my workshops and events. I get on stage and I speak and facilitate with excitement, energy, and passion. Then when I talk about our presence and how we are showing up, I suddenly change my whole energy and communication style. I become dull, bored, and show a true lack of passion and energy. It is amazing to see everyone's reaction in the room. They hate it! I do this to demonstrate why passion matters. We have something in our brains called mirror neurons. We automatically pick up the emotions of others.

Have you experienced sitting in your office when someone who has had a crappy morning has just walked in and dumped it all over the office? They have been cranky, down, or upset and the whole energy in the room has changed. I bet you have!

I am not saying passion is about jumping around the room like the Energizer Bunny or yelling at the top of your voice. Some of the most passionate leaders I know around the globe are actually introverts.

Passion is about believing in what you do, inspiring others to believe in it, and loving why you do what you do.

Simon Sinek, in his excellent book, *Start with Why*, said: *"People don't buy what you do, they buy why you do it."*

As a leader, it is vital to turn up with passion and be passionate about what you do. Okay, I am not Miss Passionate 24/7 but I always focus my mindset every day around how I can be the best and use my passion to create change and greatness in others. In turn, some days I have to do things I am not that passionate about, but I always focus on *why* I do what I do.

Also, I have worked with and met the most remarkable people; construction workers, cleaners, sales assistants, nurses, counsellors, and people who you might not think have the most fulfilling or exciting jobs, and they always find the purpose and passion around what they do.

Have you ever watched that show *Undercover Boss*? I *love* that show.

Why? It is just awesome to see these bosses – CEOs or managers – go undercover and speak to their talent on the ground. They listen and see why they love their jobs and what they do. It is always about the people and purpose. They find something about what they do that serves as a purpose and they are passionate. It shows too!

We all want to work on something we are passionate about, and we want to work with and be led by people who are passionate.

In turn, if you are finding it difficult to be passionate or have passion for what you do, what do you need to change? Think about it.

Find passion in what you do; find your why – or change it!

Win or lose, succeed or fail, it doesn't matter. Life is *way* too short not to live and lead it to the fullest with passion.

GREAT TIPS ✔

- **Find your sweet spot.**
  Purpose, passion, and talents.

- **Live each day.**
  Like your last. Life is way too short not to live it to the fullest and be passionate about it.

- **Choose to be passionate.**
  I always do this little exercise in my workshops. I turn up unmotivated and dispassionate. Everyone in the room looks at me, bewildered. I smile. I ask them how they feel. I hear things like *not good*, or *I want to go to sleep*. Passion can take will. It is surprising how, even after a bad day, willing yourself to be passionate and positive can change everything! Be passionate. It is contagious.

- **It takes a vision.**
  Vision is a clear mental picture of a preferred future. Vision produces passion with incredible intensity.

BE
PASSIONATE.
End of story.

Chapter 15

Fail Fast Move Forward

I stuff up. Sometimes my stuff-ups are small, sometimes they are huge! I love my mistakes and failings. Alright, to be honest, at the time they suck. Sometimes I even feel crap. Looking back, though, I've had my greatest insights and learnings from my fundamental mistakes. And it is okay to sometimes doubt yourself and have that fear of failure. Thing is, I don't let my self-doubt or fear stop me from trying to be the best I can be.

There are many people in history who gave it a go and were shut down. Walt Disney. The Beatles. Michael Jordan. Sonia McDonald. There have been plenty of times I wondered if the no-talent police were going to arrest me. But it never stopped me. This fear of failure and failing truly served me. It is a great motivator to be and do better, and it keeps me in check.

> **We can control our lives by controlling our perceptions.**
>
> – Bruce Lipton

I often think about Thomas Edison. I really admire him. You know, he supposedly failed over 10,000 times before he succeeded in inventing the electric light bulb. And he never, ever gave up. That's some self-belief!

That attitude really showed in the way he handled the newspaper reporter who asked him if he felt like a failure. Edison said, "Why would I feel like a failure? And why would I ever give up? I now know definitely over 9,000 ways an electric light bulb will not work. Success is almost in my grasp."

What a great attitude. We could learn so much from this man – yet it's the same man who was regarded as too stupid to learn at school. In fact, it seems Edison may have suffered from quite pronounced learning difficulties. He could read and he did – widely and often – but wasn't comfortable in the confines of school. He was 'different.'

If you sometimes feel 'different' it's okay. It's better than okay. Celebrate it!

Edison started work at age 14 and by 15 had learnt Morse code and was working with that new-fangled telegraph thing! He was in the right place to use his curiosity and imagination.

He ended up taking out 1,093 American patents in his own name, and many more around the world. His inventions changed the world. Think about what life would be like without electric light and power utilities, sound recording, or motion pictures!

In some ways, Edison is more famous for his failures than his successes. I guess that's because it makes us feel more comfortable when we make our own mistakes. If someone as brilliant as Edison wasn't bothered when he made a mistake, why should we carry on about our own? There's a huge lesson there for all of us.

I *never* let the fear of failure or failing stop me. Don't let it stop you, either.

> *Success is the ability to go from failure to failure without losing your enthusiasm.*
> — Winston Churchill

When you fail, channel it. It is okay to be angry, disappointed, or pissed off. But you can't allow yourself to wallow in it. Learn from it and keep moving.

I do this using a number of techniques. You are going to probably cringe at this but *let it go*. You heard me. Will it matter next week or next year? Reframe the situation. Ask yourself, "Am I looking at this objectively and can I maybe learn something from it?" Remember, change the frame, you change the game.

Re-label it. For instance, think: *That sucked, but maybe I could learn something.* Learn from it by thinking about what you would do differently next time. See, I can hear you saying, "I can already feel myself being more empowered by these techniques." As a leader, you can't and won't know everything. Hence … let it go!

Feel the failure. Yes, feel it. Get angry, sad, or disappointed. It is truly cool to embrace it. Do not block it out. I am not saying get angry and start throwing chairs around the office. This is where emotional intelligence, resilience, and self-regulation are important as a leader. However, it is great for the brain to feel emotions and name them. Hence when I am upset or disappointed I name it and feel it. Then I work out whether I can change, accept, or move away from the situation. And I ask myself what I would do differently or what I learned from it. Whether this learning comes from feedback, which we will look at next, or from circumstance, it's all gold in the end.

Think about your greatest learning from a failing. What was it? What difference did it make to you?

GREAT TIPS ✔

- **Love failure.**
  Yes, love it! I have had my absolute best learnings from failing. Okay, at the time they suck but there are always lessons.

- **Accept the failure.**
  Guess what, some things are *not* in your control. It is a marathon, not a sprint. Move quickly by accepting the failure and you will find you move quicker by using it as a lesson.

- **You are not alone.**
  I shared some great stories of amazing people who have failed. We have all failed. Surround yourself with people who are open about this, too.

- **Screw it.**
  Sometimes I truly believe in something, and it is not working. Then I need to screw it. Take a step back and figure out why it is failing. I breathe and let it go. Sometimes I figure it out; sometimes I move on. Don't let your fear of failing stop you from trying, taking risks, or being creative as a leader.

- *There is no failure. Only feedback.*
  I love this quote by Robert Allen. Let's explore feedback in the next chapter.

If you have

NEVER
FAILED

you have

NEVER
LIVED

Abraham Lincoln

Chapter 16
Why Feedback Doesn't Have to Suck

I love feedback. Not. Who does? Well, it is pivotal as leaders to accept and give feedback. We give most of our leaders some sort of feedback assessment or diagnostic. It helps us all look at ourselves in the mirror.

I have to laugh at myself when I start to worry about the feedback I'm about to be given. Honestly, what could someone else tell me that is as bad as I have already been telling myself? Nothing, right? But I just don't like to hear someone else say it. I don't like the thought of perhaps having let someone down or not living up to their expectations.

Where does the fear come from when we talk about being given feedback? Well, actually, it's that little voice in your head that spots an opportunity to mess with your mind, and starts up with the "You're not good enough" comments.

> **We all need people who will give us feedback. That's how we improve.**
>
> – Bill Gates

Typically, we're not great at giving feedback to others unless we've had some training. You know what it's like. You've probably heard it yourself. "Ah, you stuffed up that last job." Ouch! That's a criticism that hurts and it's not particularly constructive. Where does the conversation go from there? Probably downhill! No wonder we take feedback so personally and worry about it so much.

That's why it's so important to deliver feedback using specific examples of performance. Instead of 'you stuffed up' you might point out that the work was submitted two days late or that a certain component was overlooked. By giving specifics, you move the emphasis away from the person and onto the job. It's less confronting to hear and it channels the conversation towards areas that can actually be worked on to improve performance.

And remember to give feedback about what was done well, too. Again, be specific. The more specific you can be, the easier it will be for the person to remember and replicate those actions. You get more of the good stuff – and get it more often.

So if we actually stop and think about it, the chance to receive some honest feedback about what we're doing is a golden opportunity to learn and grow. It's all in how we look at it.

You know that voice in your head which tells you all the things you've done wrong or you could have done better? Feedback will help shut that voice up by balancing the information you have about your performance – bringing in the positives. Feedback is about what you've done well and where you need to make some improvement. You can build on your strengths while you fill in gaps in your knowledge or skills, too.

To be a truly awesome leader, you can't stand still where you are now. You've just started a lifelong process of learning and developing yourself and your skills. When you think about performance feedback, start thinking of it as a learning tool.

One of my mentors, who is brilliant at feedback, has mentored me for several years. I met him when I attended a Safety Awards ball. I sat at his table (yes, I went alone to network, which is pivotal – find out more about this in Chapter 18) and we spoke all night about leadership and my work. He gives me the most constructive and insightful feedback each and every time we meet. He always frames the feedback as coming from a good place and he has been an advisor and advocate for me and my leadership. Feedback really matters.

As Elon Musk says, "Take as much feedback from as many people as you can about whatever idea you have … Seek critical feedback. Ask them what's wrong. You often have to draw it out in a nuanced way to figure out what's wrong."

As *leader* it's your responsibility to deliver constructive feedback to your team. It's also your responsibility to show them that feedback is something to be valued, not feared.

And as an *individual,* it's your responsibility to sort through any awkwardly delivered feedback you may be given, and look for the nuggets of gold in there.

Feedback is the breakfast of champions.   – Ken Blanchard

I know that can be easier said than done, especially when life throws everything at you all at once. Yes, it has a habit of that, doesn't it?

If you need help working through the feedback or, even better, you want to tap into an honest and regular supply of performance feedback, think about working with a coach or mentor. We'll talk about that in our next chapter.

In the meantime, what are you going to do when that critical voice in your head starts up again? What can you say to yourself that will help you ignore it and start looking for the positives?

GREAT TIPS ✔

- **Seek feedback.**
  Too many people do this only once in a blue moon. Personal development is an ongoing process so that means you need feedback regularly to help you move forward. Seek feedback from people you trust, respect, and who will be honest.

- **Receive feedback thankfully.**
  It takes guts to give someone some honest feedback, so appreciate what your people are doing for you and accept feedback with thanks.

- **Take some time afterwards to reflect.**
  It will take time to work through the feedback you have been given, and to see where it applies and how. Don't rush into action. Give yourself time to think first.

- **Don't take it personally!**
  Remember, it is only feedback and sometimes you will have to take it on board – and sometimes you won't. The choice is yours.

Feedback is a GIFT

Chapter 17

Find a Coach or Mentor. Now

There is something that people who are not leaders often don't know. Being a real leader doesn't mean you always know what to do, or always get to do what you want. It also means that it is important to admit when you are stuck, and always be seeking ideas and opinions from people even higher up.

There's a saying that goes, "If you're the smartest person in the room, you are in the wrong room." While it is wonderful to be surrounded by cheerleaders, and your team should always be supportive, there is really no end to learning and personal development that can improve your business and the way you work. You might be an expert in your field, but you can still benefit from the advice of another expert, or someone who has been around a bit longer.

Who exactly seeks out a Coach? Winners.

– Chicago Tribune

Alternatively, useful viewpoints can come from a leader in another field, and the crossing over of ideas can lead to new breakthroughs.

Truly successful leaders acknowledge there is always room for improvement, and are not above asking for help. This is why the position of mentor or coach is so very important, and why every leader should be open to development throughout their careers.

But do you need a coach or a mentor? Good question.

The difference between a coach and a mentor

A coach is usually there to help you develop or master a specific set of skills or learn to manage a particular job. It's a regular session which is task-focused so it's easy to measure your progress over time. And, when you've mastered the skill or job, the coaching is no longer needed.

A mentor role is different. Mentoring is more related to personal development and often has a future focus; for example, preparing you for your next role or for a specific committee or purpose. There's a real relationship there between the mentor and mentee, and it's based on trust. You might not see your mentor on a regular basis, but he or she is always there when you need advice or guidance. This is more a long-term role, with some successful mentor relationships lasting for years.

So what do you need: specific help to do with the hands-on elements of the job, or guidance with the reasoning and understanding involved? When you know the help you need, you will know who to go to.

How do you find a coach? Easy. Look for the person who has already mastered the task. Now, this won't always be someone of a higher rank; start by looking within your team. The chances are that one of your team members is awesome at the very thing you need to learn. How stoked will they be when you ask for their help! There's a win for both of you right there.

To find a suitable mentor for you, first look within your own network. Who inspires you? Who already knows how you work and has a good sense of your potential? These people are good candidates for mentors, as they know their time will not be wasted helping you.

Keep in mind it could be a relationship in which the help goes both ways. It is likely you have the power or connections to assist your mentor too, either by referring clients, or helping spread ideas through social media. I am constantly giving back to my mentors.

For a beneficial mentorship to flourish, it is imperative to respect the time and resources that your mentor shares with you. Be careful not to give the impression that you know it all (we sometimes pull that out as a defence mechanism and don't even realise we're doing it) and don't be afraid to try new ways of doing things. Bring your creativity, and earnestly invest your time and effort preparing for and being excited about your work.

By being prepared and enthusiastic about advancement, you can learn a lot from mentors and coaches, and continue developing professionally for years.

You are capable of doing awesome things for you and your team. Now go out there and find the help you need! Start. Now.

Have you got a mentor?

Write a list of potential mentors here.

GREAT TIPS ✔

- **Don't be afraid to ask.**
  Do it! When you find the perfect person, don't be afraid to ask them to mentor you. It's an honour to be asked and you can be fairly certain they will do what they can to help you. We all love to help.

- **Ask the right way, and be coach and mentor-ready.**
  Explain why you've chosen the person as your coach or mentor. Make sure their values are aligned to you. Tell them what you want from the relationship (flattery can get you anywhere!) and what you envision as the time commitment.

- **Choose more than one mentor or coach.**
  I have several formal and informal mentors and coaches. They are all bringing something different to the relationship.

- **Give back.**
  Mentors and coaches are a must-have in your leadership and career journey. Make sure you give back to them too.

Remember to
ALWAYS
GIVE BACK

Chapter 18

Network. Network. Network.

I'm sure you've heard it before – it's not what you know, but who. Great leaders know this better than anyone, and use their networks not only for opportunities and advancement, but to strengthen their businesses and even deal with day-to-day issues without chaining themselves to their desk 24/7.

Good networking contacts provide support, feedback, resources, and even fresh information that can be applied to many different business challenges and tasks. Despite this, strategic networking is something that many aspiring leaders lack confidence in, or hate outright.

In some ways, it's easy to understand why managers shy away from networking. Most got to where they are in life by a combination of a strong command of their job and excelling at

Networking is marketing. Marketing yourself, marketing your uniqueness, marketing what you stand for.

– Christine Comaford-Lynch

personal focus and determination. When it comes time to call on someone else, especially with the hope that they may be able to come up with a better idea, or do a better job than they can themselves, most feel uncomfortable or may even reject the idea completely.

In today's fast-paced world, it seems we make friends in a heartbeat on social networks. But how many of us are really utilising these connections? Rather than simply being a time waster, looking at how social network mavens network can give us some unique insights into being successful with leadership networking.

Mark Zuckerberg, CEO of Facebook, one of the most successful social networking sites, is an expert at building relationships. From the beginning of his career, although he had few personal friends, he made sure to build connections and relationships with anyone who was someone in Silicon Valley, exactly where he wanted to achieve success. Another recent mover and shaker, Jon Levy (The Science of Influence and Adventure), is a master networker and inspirational speaker. He's used networking heavily to rise from a relative nobody to great success in his field.

So how do you create a network like Zuckerberg's or Levy's? The first fundamental step is to surround yourself with people who are successful and driven themselves. But you need to recognise that they likely have hundreds of other demands on their time. The real first step then is to work out what you can offer a potential connection, without thinking of what you could get in return. Offer value without expectation and you offer a networking opportunity people will desire.

Once you do meet someone you want to connect with on a deeper level, make yourself memorable, and remember what's important to them. Keep away from shop talk for as long as possible, and get to know your contact personally. By doing this you're more likely to attract people that genuinely like you and will want to help you in the future.

Get to know the gatekeepers. Busy entrepreneurs and leaders will likely have someone assisting with their schedules and communications. It's often said you can learn a lot about someone by the way they treat others, so be polite and respectful to all staff members you encounter and you'll be treated with respect yourself when trying to reach the influencer you'd like to network with.

Lastly, don't be afraid to reach out. Skip the sales talk and keep your first contact as short as possible, but don't be afraid to let them know you think what they're doing is fascinating and you'd like to get to know more about it and them. Include a clear next step and make it easy for the contact to get in touch with you if they're interested. If you do meet up with them, remember to send a follow-up thank you note or email sooner rather than later, and then build the relationship from there.

By building a strong leadership network you'll be equipping yourself with a core group of like-minded professionals who can extend both your professional and personal reach for years to come.

The currency of real networking is not greed but generosity.

— Keith Ferrazzi

GREAT TIPS ✔

- **Make networking your friend.**
  Do it! Make networking part of your leadership and career strategy.

- **Plan and research your networking.**
  Networking for the sake of networking doesn't work. Make sure you have a plan and research the right places to network. Networking with purpose, and planning to network in places with a common interest and passion, are always more effective.

- **Connect and give back.**
  Don't attend networking events just to collect business cards. It is important to really connect, get to know people, and give back.

- **Online networking.**
  It is vital you have a great online profile and presence. In turn you are networking and connecting with people who you can help, support, or collaborate with.

- **Follow up.**
  This is important. Remember to send a note or email thanking the people you meet. No one does this, and you can really stand out.

Make networking

YOUR
FRIEND

Chapter 19

Focus on Your Tribe

Guess what? We were born to connect; we are a connection machine, and our brains are social organs! Connecting as a leader is pivotal.

We all have people around us who want to help row our boat. We don't need thousands of people on Facebook or millions of contacts; we do need true friends, supporters, associates, and people who want to help and support us to be the best we can be. These people are your true tribe – your real supporters. As they care for us, we in turn must take care of them. It is about *giving*, not receiving.

I really love supporting and caring for my tribe. Successful people have a great support network; make sure they are great by giving them your whole attention!

> **You are truly home only when you find your tribe.**
>
> – Srividya Srinivasan

All of us have supporters in our lives who are willing to help us achieve our goals. Some of these people are found among our family members, our neighbours, and our closest friends. Others we may have met at school, our workplace, or through a shared activity or interest in our community. Because of the power of the Internet it's possible to develop close, vibrant relationships with those we haven't even met face-to-face.

Regardless of the physical distance between us, or how these people come into our lives, these are the people we share a common bond with. We share values and ideas, and we speak the same language. We have trust and mutual respect for one another. These are the people that get us and we get them. These are the people we all have around us who want to help row our boat, who we can count on through good and bad times. These people are our people; they are our tribe!

Have You Found Your Tribe?

Being a member of a tribe is a little like being part of a large, extended family. In a healthy family unit, members come together to build one another up, support one another, and defend each other. When you are around your other tribe members, you will find that you feel encouraged, energised, and renewed. You feel as though you can meet any challenge head on, and overcome any and all obstacles.

When you find your tribe and gain their trust and support, you will discover that it is suddenly much easier to achieve your goals in your life. With their help, it's now possible to make your vision for the future a reality. All of these things are much harder, if not impossible, without the full support of your tribe.

Your Tribe Needs You!

Just as you need to find your tribe, your tribe needs you. Tribes follow and support a specific leader because they believe in this person. Even if it remains unspoken, tribes follow the person they believe shares their values and who will listen to them. Tribes follow the leader they feel is in the best position to protect them and look out for their interests, while also helping to nudge and move the tribe forward towards a common, shared goal.

In the media, we hear a lot of talk about the need for leaders to establish their authority and build their following. We are told over and over by various pundits that it is important to get as many followers as possible so that we can steer conversations and influence opinions in order to direct change.

There are now thousands of CEOs and leaders in government and other institutions turning to social media to share their thoughts and get their message out. And people follow them online by the millions. From Martha Stewart and Oprah Winfrey to Tim Cook, Bill Gates, and Seth Godin, millions follow these leaders on their Twitter and Facebook accounts.

While it can be great to have a large following on social media, the truth of the matter is that you don't need a large following in order to be a great leader, effect change, and achieve your goals. We don't need to have tens of thousands of people on Facebook or millions of contacts in order to change ourselves or the world. To be a great leader, and to be able to achieve our goals, we just need to find our tribe. We just need to find our true friends; supporters, associates, and people who want to help and support us to be the best we can be.

Understand your role as leader and your responsibility to your tribe – take care of your tribe!

Being the leader of a tribe is about more than just seeking out and securing the help and support of others; being the leader of a tribe is a great responsibility. In turn, we also must take care of our tribe. Leadership is about *giving,* not receiving.

Have you found your tribe?

Are you taking care of your tribe?

Are you listening to your tribe and finding out what is important to them, and discovering what their needs are and how you can best help them?

Are you standing up for them and supporting their issues so that they will later stand for you and support yours?

Are you using your communication skills to encourage your tribe and help them to connect with each other as well as to connect with members and leaders of other tribes that share your values and vision for the future?

Are you giving your tribe what they need to grow and thrive and be the best version of themselves that they can be?

I really love supporting and caring for my tribe. Successful people have a great support network. They take the time to build their tribe. It takes time to build bonds of trust and respect and create an environment where cooperation and collaboration can flourish. Take the time to find your tribe.

Seek out the people who share your values, ideas, and vision for the future and who energise you and increase your happiness. Surround yourself with them. Use your communication skills to strengthen your bonds with them and give them what they need to grow and become better people. Stand up for them and look out for their interests. Listen to them, make certain their needs are being met, and make sure they are great!

GREAT TIPS ✔

- **Put yourself out there.**
  Don't be afraid to open yourself up to new experiences and people. It is amazing where you will find people who will form part of your tribe.

- **Be mindful in your intention-setting.**
  When you're ready to find your tribe, put it out there! Set clear intentions on why, who, and what you want and need.

- **It is okay to be weird and vulnerable.**
  Recently I met someone who is an amazing leader and entrepreneur. She is such a great supporter of mine and really helps lift me up. I told her I love having her in my life and part of my tribe. Yes, I felt weird and vulnerable telling her this. After meeting her through a product she created for me, I knew she rocked. Weird is good.

- **Surround yourself with like-minded individuals.**
  My tribe is filled with truly amazing leaders and entrepreneurs. They have great values and energy. Surround yourself with people who get you and your why, will give you honest and open advice and feedback, and help you be the best.

- **Ditch judgment.**
  I love meeting different people. We are all different and unique. We are all special. It does not mean we are more special than others though. Everyone in my tribe brings different ways of thinking. Ditch the judgment, embrace the differences.

- **Let go.**
  Let go of people in your tribe who are putting holes in your boat. This is hard but there are people in your tribe who were there for a reason and sometimes you need to let them go. Do it.

- **Don't be shy. Take action.**
  It can take a bit of nerve to tell someone why you admire them. Don't let shyness stop you. Be brave and speak up. You will come out a winner.

SURROUND YOURSELF
with your tribe

Chapter 20

Empower Others to Lead

At the heart of every successful leader is not their charisma or even their skill. Instead, what sets a great leader apart is their ability to encourage and empower others to step up and lead themselves. Originally, it was thought that what made a great leader was the ability to maintain complete control over any situation, and to direct their will to others. You may even still think this today; however today's best leaders – in multiple industries from manufacturing to Silicon Valley – know that they are at their most effective when they empower others to take the reins, too.

To create the kind of culture in your workplace where employees feel comfortable in stepping forward with their own plans and ideas is deceptively simple – focus on relationships first and business requirements second.

As we look ahead into the next century, leaders will be those who empower others.

– Bill Gates

Experts agree that if you take care of the people first, then the rest will take care of itself. Giving staff members the opportunity to take the lead themselves gives them greater purpose in their role and also opens up the input and ideas across an entire project.

One of the best examples of a leader who empowers others is Tony Hsieh of Zappos. He believes in putting relationships ahead of business, and empowering his people to lead.

He said, "Our number one priority is company culture. Our whole belief is that if you get the culture right, most of the other stuff like delivering great customer service or building a long-term enduring brand will just happen naturally on its own."

And when asked in an interview on the leadership blog, *Executive Street,* what his number one priority as CEO was, he answered, "Thinking about how I can empower my employees to be a part of the growth and innovation of the company."

He believes the future is about self-management, and that can't happen unless people are empowered to think for themselves and lead others when appropriate.

His thinking moved Zappos from being an online shoe-selling business to a $1 billion company that was eventually acquired by Amazon. Not bad for a business that simply changed its culture, is it?

So how can you encourage this culture in your business?

Bill George gives us the following advice in his book *Discover Your True North.*

GREAT TIPS ✔

- **Treat others as equals.**
  From the janitor to the CEO, everyone has a place in a business and deserves respect. By approaching people in a friendly and authentic way, you give them space to respond in turn.

- **Really listen.**
  Active listening is one of the most important traits of a good leader. When someone senses that you are genuinely interested in them and what they have to say, they will be encouraged to share more openly. We are innately an excellent judge of when someone is really interested in what we have to say. Use this to your advantage.

- **Everyone has something to teach us.**
  Just as we feel accepted when someone takes our opinion into account, it's important to remember that everyone we meet will have something new to teach us as well. Everyone has a different perspective and brings different strengths to the table. All staff, young and old, have valid experiences worth learning from.

- **Share stories.**
  This is a critical part of relationship building and it helps create the culture around you. By being real and authentic, you create trust. Telling stories of your wins and losses, your life, your dreams … they all form part of the connections that bind you together. If your team members feel comfortable to open up and share their stories together, it's a clear sign that they feel empowered and valued, as well as safe.

- **Tell everyone the big picture.**
  When everyone in your organisation knows your core business message, and what you're trying to achieve, they can all work collectively towards those goals. When your expectations and goals are clear it becomes that much easier for staff to align their own work towards those goals. It's not easy, but creating a positive workplace culture is well worth the effort.

  By creating a work environment where people are encouraged and supported to express their own ideas, make decisions, and try new ideas and paths, you'll be building a business with the strongest base. When you have an entire team of leaders all moving in the same direction, the business's momentum will be hard to beat.

A leader is best when people barely know he exists, when his work is done, his aim fulfilled, they will say: we did it ourselves. — Lao Tzu

Be the ripple effect.

EMPOWER OTHERS.

Chapter 21

Great Leaders Never Stop Learning

If you are reading this book, you are committed to learning! You are committed to being the best you can be. Bring it on!

The continual pursuit of excellence is one of the key traits that help good leaders become great. A great leader is always learning something new, every single day, because great leaders never lose their hunger to grow and their passion to improve.

I believe that the following quote by acting legend Jack Nicholson expresses why great leaders never stop learning.

The minute that you're not learning I believe you're dead.

When we lose our passion to improve, when we abandon our quest for excellence, we stop learning. When we stop

> **Leadership and learning are indispensable to each other.**
>
> — John F. Kennedy

learning, it really is as though an integral part of our inner core has died. We become complacent. We stop growing and we lose the ability to understand and influence others. When we stop learning, we stop leading. When we stop learning we are literally stuck.

We stop moving. We are dead in the water.

I am passionate about leadership. I don't want to settle for good enough, I strive for greatness! But funnily enough, as passionate as I am about leadership, and as much as I work in the leadership space, I don't call myself an expert. I consider myself a semi-expert because I am still growing, I am still hungry to improve, and I never want to stop learning.

As silly as this might sound to some, I freely admit my flaws. Despite my past successes, I don't know everything – nor do I want to!

Being honest with ourselves, admitting what we do not know, and remaining open to learning has a number of benefits. Whether it's chasing down the root issue in a complex process that's holding back the performance; taking the time to learn more about the world at large; or simply picking up a new skill; the act of learning has the same effect on our brains as lifting weights does for the muscles in our bodies.

Learning opens our minds and thought processes up to new ways of viewing the world and the people in it. It literally keeps us sharp and on our toes and provides a boost to our self-esteem and energy when we achieve mastery. Learning provides a wellspring for greater creativity and innovation. We have greater insight, an increased ability to solve problems, and we become more valuable to ourselves, our company, and the people in our lives. As others see our hunger and drive to improve ourselves through learning, it creates a culture that encourages others to seek more opportunities for growth and development.

Are you still growing, or are you stuck? Do you still have a passion to learn and improve, do you still have your drive for excellence, or do you sometimes feel as though you are spinning your wheels and you are unable to move forward to the next level?

A great leader will never settle for just getting by and getting through the day. They understand that they don't know everything – that they can't know everything – and they aren't afraid to admit it. With leadership training you can stop settling for good enough and learn the skills that you need to help you move forward and embrace your greatness!

How can you continue to have a leader's mindset?

GREAT TIPS ✔

- **You don't know everything.**
  Research has shown the best leaders are the ones who practise self-development. Do it!

- **Trust that you'll adapt to new challenges.**
  Successful leaders approach uncertainty with confidence and an open mind to learning.

- **Believe in your individuality.**
  I know I carry on about this one. Every successful leader champions their individuality. Own who you are and why you rock. This takes continual learning.

- **Question your negative beliefs.**
  You don't have to believe what you believe! Question your negative beliefs and you'll soon find the holes in them. You know you can do this and have a positive and growing mindset. Always.

NEVER STOP LEARNING

Chapter 22

Significance and Success

One day I was working on a major construction site. It was early in my consulting career and for some reason I took a moment to stand in the midst of the activity on site to reflect. At the time, I had just returned from living overseas, and was starting my life over again. I didn't have the fancy car or house, I bought my clothes on eBay or at second-hand stores, and I didn't go out very much. But I stood there and realised how successful I had become. I was successful because I was significant to others.

Leadership is not about money; leadership is about vision, significance, and making a difference.

Do you deem yourself successful?

If so, how have you come to that conclusion?

> **What will matter is not your success but your significance.**
>
> — Michael Josephson

Often, success is defined as having a lot of money or being rich in material possessions. Although some may predetermine the dollar figure that will define them as successful, having this as the focus tends to keep people wanting, and never actually feeling they have achieved success, even after they've reached the amount.

Success, really, can be defined in so many different ways. It is a very subjective term. Financial success, or having an income of over a certain amount, is merely one of the ways that *contribute* to your success. It doesn't define you, however, or determine whether or not you're successful.

As a leader, you're probably already aware that success comes in different shapes and forms. Completing a project on time and within budget, for example, gives you an amazing lift. Persistently and consistently achieving this outcome makes you a success.

Successfully leading a team to this outcome also shows you're a success in your field. You can navigate and negotiate not only a range of personalities and diverse skills and talents, but can do so without losing your team's respect or focus on the final outcome.

There's a further element outside of achieving goals and deadlines, and leading a team, however. The difference you make to your client, their customers or clients, and the outcome in general will also determine how successful you are.

How you lead, and how you leave others feeling in your wake, are all indicators of achievement. Money is only a small part of it and in many cases, despite how much more they can buy, it often doesn't leave people feeling any sense of achievement, much less a success.

It's the changes you make to someone's life as a result of the work, and the leading you do, which will give you the most fulfilment. That will leave you feeling successful, knowing you have done something important with your life.

You have made a significant difference to someone's life. No amount of money can beat that.

Yes, you can do it. You can be significant and successful, and in the next chapter you will see that you can plan for success, but sometimes the first steps seem to happen almost by accident. But, in reality, you have made up your mind and focused, so you create serendipity ...

How can you be significant to others?

If your actions inspire others to dream more, learn more, do more and become more, you are a leader. — John Quincy Adams

GREAT TIPS ✔

- **Work toward being significant.**
  If you want to have success, you can't make success your goal. As Oprah says, the key is not to worry about being successful, but to instead work toward being significant – and the success will naturally follow.

- **Make a difference.**
  Think back to leaders or people who have made a difference in your life. How can you pay it forward? This is leadership. Be significant.

- **Be a cheerleader.**
  Cheer on your team, tribe, and those people around you that need your support and encouragement. It will matter significantly to them.

- **Do good.**
  Always lead with your heart (and head) and with good intention. It will swing back tenfold.

SIGNIFICANCE MATTERS

Chapter 23

Serendipity and Curiosity

You have to love unexpected accidents or happenings. I love surprises. If you don't love surprises maybe skip this chapter. Just kidding! It is really about opportunities as a leader and being completely curious about life.

Serendipity means a 'happy accident' or 'pleasant surprise' yet the authors of the book *Get Lucky*, Thor Muller and Lane Becker, argue that we can plan for serendipity simply by activating the part of our brain which deals with curiosity.

Curiosity opens the mind up so that it is receptive to new things going on around it. In fact, the authors say successful people are good at taking advantage of chance happenings that occur throughout their life.

There is no such thing as accident; it is fate misnamed.

– Napoleon Bonaparte

They say, "Planned serendipity is not an abstract, magical notion. It's a practical skill."

I believe that my curious brain was at work planning serendipity when I arranged to meet the Pro Chancellor of the Queensland University of Technology (QUT). We had met a few months prior at a *neuroscience of leadership* summit and I wanted to take the opportunity to meet him as a thought leader in business and leadership, and talk with him about leadership.

I didn't know at the time that he would invite me to the QUT Business Leaders Ball for 800 people that night, where they would be inducting some Hall of Fame leaders.

| *I have no special talents. I am only passionately curious.* — Albert Einstein

I arrived not knowing where I was sitting. I sat with a table of 10 senior executives and was feeling pretty special because I was right at the front of the room. I introduced myself to the people around the table and started speaking to the CEO of a leading mining company about the wonderful and complex world of leadership.

Upon speaking further with this CEO, it became apparent – and this was so coincidental – that I would actually be meeting his head of human resources that very next day. Serendipity …

The next day, I met the head of HR and he told me that his CEO had come in that morning and said that he must take time to really meet me and listen to what I had to say. I was a little humbled … we chatted for ages about my gifts, dreams, and why I am so passionate about what I do.

He said, "Your story is inspirational and you are a role model for women. I want to see how you can share that same passion with the women in my organisation." *Wow!*

It was that seed that gave me the idea to see what a great 'woman in a leadership' program would look like, and see if I could do it? Of course I could! And I did! I opened myself up to opportunities and I was curious about them. The best things can happen when they are not expected. Some of the best products, programs, ideas, and companies have been developed, born, and created due to serendipity and curiosity.

Think about it. I had a happy accident – serendipity – but unless I had taken a chance in the first place, nothing would have ever happened. This is what the authors of *Get Lucky* mean by planned serendipity. You don't need luck; you need to be ready to take advantage of chances as they pop up.

I also want to explore the notion of being totally able to explore opportunities: that dream job, a great promotion, whatever that thing is that lands in your lap. Why do you feel you have to tick *every* box before you do it, go for it, and take it?

Come on! Explore it. Be curious. Take it. Even if you *only* tick seven out of the 10 boxes, go for it! Don't you want to be challenged? Learn something? Grow? Open your mind to possibilities and go for it.

Did I know how to run a women in leadership program completely? No! But I gave it a go. I made some mistakes. It rocked. I learnt how to make it better. It is still evolving. But I said yes. I opened myself for opportunities.

And you know what else I did? I *asked!* To this day, I ask. I ask people who I want to meet and learn from to go for coffee – once I asked a CEO of a $2 billion company for coffee and he ended up being my mentor for a few years. Great stuff!

Don't be afraid to ask or to go for what you really want. If you get a *no*, ask the next person or go for the next opportunity. Don't take *no* as an answer. Take *no* as an opportunity for something or someone else more amazing to come into your world. Allow serendipity and curiosity to take over.

When you open up your mind to possibilities, say *yes* to opportunities, and are curious about what could be, you never know what might happen ... you might create your own serendipity!

Think about serendipity in your life. What happy accidents have you experienced?

- **Be audacious!**
  Success and significance tend to favour the bold and curious. So be it! Make sure you set a remarkable leadership vision that challenges you. A big vision and the ability to think with curiosity will open you up to the action that creates serendipity.

- **Do it now.**
  Do not wait. Want serendipity? Be curious. You need to act! Bump into things. Make it happen.

- **Remember the fail fast.**
  Just fail fast. Get up. Learn. Grow. And take a different or slightly adjusted action. Repeat. Leaders make mistakes; they fail. We are all different, and we all share one thing in common; we all fail. Do it fast. And we all can share wonderful stories of serendipity coming from failing, too.

- **Be positive.**
  Yes, yes, yes! Be the leader who is glass half-full. Be a leader who is always looking for the upside and you will absolutely find more serendipity. It is just a reality of life.

- **Say *yes* as a default.**
  It is amazing what can happen by saying *yes*.

BE CURIOUS.
Every day.

Chapter 24

You Lead Our World

I remember taking a leap of faith in myself and focusing on my passion and purpose – and what made me different! I owned that difference to start LeadershipHQ. It took courage, passion, determination, and guts to do this. To not compete or be like anyone else. To be just me. Just different. And there have been times where that difference has been applauded and celebrated, and other times where it was judged and criticised.

We are not born to judge, discriminate, or hate someone because they are different. We learn this. We can also learn to love, respect, and care for everyone in spite of the differences.

I remember Martin Luther King, Jr., saying, "I have a dream; I have a dream that my four little children will one day live in a nation where they

> **Great leadership usually starts with a willing heart, a positive attitude, and a desire to make a difference.**
>
> – Mac Anderson

will not be judged by the colour of their skin but by the content of their character."

The thing is, even though we have made progress, we still seem to be playing the same game now. We have just found 100 different ways to play it.

I have a dream, too, but I want a world where we are not having the diversity debate or discussion. It is not about race, disability, gender, or age. It is about appreciating that we have a world of 7.3 billion humans where we are each different. We celebrate uniqueness and 7.3 billion people's diversity of thought.

> I want a world where diversity and inclusion are just naturally a part of business.
>
> Instead of 'it starts with me', it starts with 'we'.
>
> Instead of 'gender intelligence', we see intelligence in all.
>
> I want a world where we know that creativity and innovation are within each one of us.
>
> A world where we feel truly safe for authentically being who we are.
>
> A world where we see you, truly see you!

I want us not to commit to the *word* 'diversity' but to the *action* of embracing our differences.

Since going on my journey, taking a leap of faith to start my own company, I focused on what was unique and different about me, and I owned it. I owned my difference. I'm not perfect. None of us are, but it is our imperfections that make us real. We may have disabilities, but they are what give us the ability to be our unique selves.

I ask you, what are we really doing about diversity? Are we hard-wired to see what we want to see, no matter what we are? Or can we do something about it?

What if we could lead everyone toward the ideal world?

What if we could show people what the world looks like when diversity is not the buzzword, but part of how we live? What if we could model in our language and actions such things as acceptance, appreciation of difference, and the value of the unique, human respect, inclusivity, and vulnerability?

What if we could lead people to a world where there was no judgment, and we are truly seen for how we are, respected and being respectful?

This is my dream.

I invite everyone to stop the conversation and take action. Stop the debates and start showing up as the leaders we are.

We are all capable of experiencing and learning to enjoy this brand new world, but not everyone is able to take us there.

The world won't change while we talk about it. We can only create a world where it is safe to be who we are if we start leading and showing the way.

If you and I don't do it, who will?

I see and lead that world ... You lead *our* world. We lead *our* world.

How can you start to lead our world?

GREAT TIPS ✔

- **Create your legacy now.**
  Think about how you want to be remembered. Leadership starts with you.

- **Do not judge.**
  It is easy to make assumptions about others. Assumptions based on our beliefs and biases. Be open and inclusive to everyone around us.

- **Practise inclusiveness.**
  We are all different. Embrace it. We do not have to agree with everyone as they have their own assumptions, beliefs, and thoughts. The best leaders are open to diversity of thoughts – be inclusive.

- **Make them feel safe.**
  The brain's number one role is to keep us safe from threat. Make them feel safe inside and out. Make them feel safe to be truly who they are.

- **Be the change you want to be and see.**
  If you want a world where there is a change, lead the way.

WE LEAD our WORLD

Chapter 25

Jump Off the Cliff

Last year I had some massive and heartbreaking challenges. It truly affected my leadership. We have all been there. Life happens. The one thing that helped me greatly was my ability to be vulnerable and have the courage to ask for help. I truly see power in vulnerability. Many see it as a weakness. I don't. Being vulnerable literally made me feel like I was jumping off a cliff.

To be the leader you want to be, you need to be seen, truly seen. Being a leader is not easy. You need to take risks. Ask for help. You will fail. Sometimes you will fall.

Fear. Shame. Disappointment. Guilt. Embarrassment. What do these words mean to you? To me, they mean vulnerability. They are feelings and words many of us don't want to feel

Authenticity is a collection of choices that we have to make every day.
It's about the choice to show up and be real.
The choice to be honest.
The choice to let our true selves be seen.

– Brené Brown

or express. Thing is, when we numb these feelings, we numb wonderful feelings such as joy, happiness, love, and kindness as well. We can't just numb the bad ones. When we do, we also automatically numb the good.

However, they don't need to be seen through that lens. Let me explore another perspective on vulnerability through a neuroscience lens.

First, I am going to share a story where I am going to be slightly vulnerable myself. I remember standing on this cliff … Okay, it wasn't actually a cliff, but it felt like one when I was thinking of following my dreams and starting a business. I felt such fear. I was anxious and apprehensive. I was totally vulnerable. What happens if I fail? Maybe I won't be good enough. These were real and constant thoughts running through my brain. But I did it anyway!

Why was being in a state of vulnerability such a powerful feeling for me?

Since then, it has actually been at the forefront of all the work I do, whether it is leading a team; making a presentation to the board; failing in a project; or even dealing with an angry customer. This can be scary stuff. It doesn't have to be, when we reframe it or look at it from another perspective.

Vulnerability is power.

If it wasn't for vulnerability, ultimately I would not have jumped off that cliff. I would not have looked vulnerability in the face and said "Guess what, I am going to serve my purpose and I am going to make a difference. I am going to show up and be seen. I am going to focus my thoughts, creativity, and innovation on using the power vulnerability gives me to contribute in my work and with my leaders."

This isn't easy though. Vulnerability activates the parts of the brain that basically want us to run and hide. That lizard part of the brain, which focuses on keeping you alive. Vulnerability can be pain, fear, or even trauma. It can activate the same parts of the brain that make us feel as if someone is physically punching us. Ouch! This in turn activates the threat response in the brain, which hinders our rational thinking and produces a not-so-nice stress chemical called cortisol.

The great news (thank goodness) is that by understanding neuroscience and how it works in relation to vulnerability, we can create environments and techniques not only for ourselves but also for those around us. As leaders, we can use the power of vulnerability to create environments and teams that are open to change, creativity, and innovation. Imagine how powerful and effective you and your team would be if they embraced vulnerability.

Luckily the brain can be your best ally in this situation. Brené Brown – my favourite speaker and author in this area – says, "Vulnerability is not about fear and grief and disappointment. It's the birthplace of everything we're hungry for: joy, creativity, faith, love, spirituality. And the whole thing is, there is no innovation and creativity without failure."

In an interview for *Forbes* magazine she goes on to say, "When you shut down vulnerability, you shut down opportunity." In her opinion, entrepreneurship and leadership is all about vulnerability.

Possibly one of the most difficult parts of being a leader is learning to allow yourself to be vulnerable and learning how to model that for your team. I don't blame anyone for being afraid when they let their guard down. Not everyone is going to understand what you are doing, or why, and not everyone will be willing to follow your example.

As leader, you need to create an environment in which it is safe for your team members to expose their vulnerabilities.

The hippocampus is the part of your brain which involves memory and learning. It helps us put situations into context, based on our experiences, so we know how to react and when it's okay to express our vulnerability. It's the hippocampus which will help you overcome fear by drawing on the memory of similar circumstances in which you managed yourself well.

What that means for leaders is that you may need to build opportunities for success into the process of exploring vulnerability. It means that you may need to help your team members notice what is happening to them during those moments of vulnerability. The more mindful they are during those moments, the more information is stored in the hippocampus, to be drawn on later, as they need it.

A trait, which seems to be a weakness, is actually a strength.

In turn, by creating this environment, you are activating parts of the brain where trust, engagement and connection are truly working. Ultimately, when our brains are operating in this environment, they produce the powerful chemical oxytocin for love and bonding. And the brain wants more of it. Amazing stuff.

Imagine a team which is strong enough to show vulnerability, and which is confident enough to be creative, loyal, adaptable, and focused. It's a team in which each member has learnt to trust themselves in the face of risk, and to learn from every experience. It starts with you – and what vulnerability means to you.

How can you be truly seen?

GREAT TIPS ✔

- **You are human.**
  Remember this always. We are all human.

- **Ask for help.**
  Believe me, this is challenging. My greatest lesson last year, as a leader, was to ask for help. It is powerful when it happens. It is amazing to see how people step up.

- **Say how you feel.**
  Have the conversation. Say what you want and need. Life is too short not to.

- **Do not worry about what people think of you.**
  It is none of your business anyway. They are too worried about their own internal struggles.

- **Vulnerability takes courage.**
  Be courageous and do it. Take small steps each day.

- **Forget being perfect.**
  It is our imperfections that make us perfect. There is no perfect leader.

there is

POWER

in Vulnerability

Chapter 26

Be the Leader *You* Want to Be

I believe we have made leadership bigger than it really is. Leadership is a mindset, behaviour, and action.

We are and can all be leaders in this world. If you have not yet watched the TED Talk called *Leading with Lollipops* by Drew Dudley, please do. No, I am not going to tell you about it here. I don't want to dilute the message that you need to hear. Go on. Go watch the video on your computer, then come back here.

What I will say is that he and I agree … Leadership is an attitude.

Leadership is about making a difference.

Leadership is about lollipop moments. Moments where we are creating a difference.

> **To help others develop, start with yourself.**
>
> – Marshal Goldsmith

Marianne Williamson once said, "Our deepest fear is not that we are inadequate. Our deepest fear is that we are powerful beyond measure. It is our Light, not our Darkness, that most frightens us."

Be the light. Own it. You are a leader.

Leadership can be learnt.

We don't learn how to walk by reading a manual on walking. We learn by actually walking, tripping over things, falling on our face, and getting back up again and again. There is no right way to learn such things, especially leadership. You must find *your* own way; that is, putting into action who you are as a leader. Leadership steps.

See yourself as a leader. *Now.* Be brave. Leadership is about courage.

This is what I would tell my younger self.

Yes, it takes courage to start looking at yourself differently, and you have to be brave to follow through with action. But if you don't do it now, when will you?

It's what you do now that matters. Today. Right here.

At the start of this book I said that leadership is an attitude. By now you will get what I mean. It's the way you see yourself, the way you see the leadership role and the way you interact with people around you. It's in what you want and how you plan to get it. It's in how you take your people along the journey with you, and achieve success together.

When you first start out as a leader, people *will* question you. "What on earth are you doing that for?"

But you know, that's a good thing. It's a sign that you're doing something different. You're doing something no one else is doing. And that's why you are a leader. You've listened and you've learnt, and now you're applying those skills that make you inspirational. You're the one with the guts to be different.

This has to be one of my favourite quotes by Coco Chanel: "In order to be irreplaceable, one must always be different."

Be different. Be authentically you. Be the leader you want to be.

I want you to reflect back on this book and see this as a journey to your destination of leadership. Keep the target and end result in mind – you are a leader. Do not focus on the process to get there; focus on your mindset and attitude as a leader. I want you to enjoy and love the journey of self-discovery of being a leader every day. You have got this.

You've got leadership attitude.

And that's why you're going to totally rock this whole leadership thing.

Let's go change the world together.

LEADERSHIP
is an
ATTITUDE

Resources

Achor, Shawn – *Is happiness the secret of success?*
  https://www.linkedin.com/pulse/happiness-secret-success-shawn-achor
Brown, Brené – *The Power of Vulnerability*
  https://www.ted.com/talks/Brené_brown_on_vulnerability
Brown, Brené – *The Gifts of Imperfection: Let Go of Who You Think You're Supposed to Be and Embrace Who You Are*
Copland, Laura – *Staff Voices: Changing Your Brain Can Change Your Mind – Why Neuroscience Matters*
  http://deploymentpsych.org/members/education/cdp-blog-content/staff-voices-content/staff-voices-changing-your-brain-can-change-your-mind-why-neuroscience-matters
Cotter Davis, Dr Rachel – quoted in *What Neuroscience Teaches Us About Change Management*
  https://www.laserfiche.com/ecmblog/what-neuroscience-teaches-us-about-change-management/
Csikszentmihalyi, Mihaly – *Creativity: Flow and the Psychology of Discovery and Invention*
  http://www.wired.com/1996/09/czik/
  http://www.amazon.com/Creativity-The-Psychology-Discovery-Invention/dp/0062283251

Cuddy, Amy – *Your Body Language Shapes Who You Are*
http://www.ted.com/talks/amy_cuddy_your_body_language_
shapes_who_you_are

Cuddy, Amy J.C., Wilmuth, Caroline A., & Carney, Dana R. – *The Benefit of Power Posing Before a High-Stakes Social Evaluation*
https://dash.harvard.edu/bitstream/handle/1/9547823/13-027.
pdf?sequence=1

Dudley, Drew – *Leading With Lollipops* TEDX Toronto
https://www.youtube.com/watch?v=hVCBrkrFrBE

Ferriss, Tim – *The 4-hour Workweek*

FitzSimons, P. – *Nancy Wake: Biography* HarperCollins – AU

Furley, P., Dicks, M., & Memmert, D. – *"Nonverbal behavior in soccer: the influence of dominant and submissive body language on the impression formation and expectancy of success of soccer players*
http://europepmc.org/abstract/med/22356883

George, Bill – *Discover Your True North*
http://www.billgeorge.org/page/true-north

Gladwell, Malcolm – *Outliers*
http://gladwell.com/outliers/

Godin, Seth – *The Tribes We Lead*
https://www.ted.com/talks/seth_godin_on_the_tribes_we_lead

Goleman, Daniel – *What Makes a Leader?*
https://hbr.org/2004/01/what-makes-a-leader

Goleman, Daniel (1995) – Cited in John O. Dozier (2010)
The Weeping, the Window, the Way, p. 130

Kabat-Zinn, J. – Quoted in *Being mindful improves leadership*
http://research.wpcarey.asu.edu/management-
entrepreneurship/being-mindful-improves-leadership

Lea, Wendy – *Who Needs Luck? Try Planned Serendipity*
http://www.inc.com/wendy-lea/forget-luck-try-planned-
serendipity.html

Muller, T. & Becker, L. – *Get Lucky*
http://www.amazon.com/Get-Lucky-Planned-Serendipity-Business/dp/1118249755

Rath, Tom – *Strengths Finder 2.0*
http://strengths.gallup.com/110440/About-StrengthsFinder-20.aspx

Schawbel, Dan – *Brené Brown: How Vulnerability Can Make Our Lives Better*
http://www.forbes.com/sites/danschawbel/2013/04/21/Brené-brown-how-vulnerability-can-make-our-lives-better/#344a9bc60bac

Sinek, Simon – *Start With Why*
https://www.startwithwhy.com/

Su, A.J. & Wilkins, M. M. – *Own the Room*
http://www.amazon.com/Own-Room-Discover-Signature-Leadership/dp/1422183939

Zenger, Jack – *"Strengths-Based Approach" Key to Building Leadership Capacity in Today's Workplace*
http://rhresources.com/strengths-based-approach-key-to-building-leadership-capacity-in-todays-workplace/

Zenger, Jack – *New Research: To Reach Full Work Potential, Hone In On Your Strengths*
http://www.forbes.com/sites/jackzenger/2015/03/06/new-research-to-reach-full-work-potential-hone-in-on-your-strengths/#2145d2ac1d95

For you, from Sonia

Thank you for reading *Leadership Attitude*. It means the world to me.

If you are planning on taking your leadership career to the next level, now is the time!

What are you waiting for?

SPECIAL OFFER

As a special thank you to you for reading this book, Sonia would like to offer you free access to the LeadershipHQ Ebook (valued at $19.97) when you subscribe to the LeadershipHQ newsletter at leadershiphq.com.au/freebook

Other important steps in your leadership journey:

- Visit the Leadership HQ (www.leadershiphq.com.au) website and explore the content on our blog.

- Investigate the wide range of services we offer, including leadership diagnostics and assessments, leadership and cultural strategies, leadership coaching, leadership programs, leadership events and workshops, leadership platinum online resources, and speaking services.

- You can also subscribe to LeadershipHQ Magazine (www.leadershiphq.com.au/register) to stay up to date with latest trends and information.

- You might like to connect with us on your preferred social media platform, and join in the conversation. Find us using the links below and use the 'like' button to stay in touch.

  - www.facebook.com/soniamcdonald01/

  - www.facebook.com/leadershiphq/

  - www.instagram.com/soniamcdonald1/

  - www.instagram.com/leadershiphq/

  - twitter.com/LeadershipHQ1

  - twitter.com/soniamcdonald01/

  - au.linkedin.com/in/soniamcdonald

Speaker

Sonia McDonald is a fun, dynamic and vibrant speaker at conferences, business events, professional development programs and more. She specialises in the neuroscience of leadership, and transforming leaders from process-focused to people-oriented. Great leaders are above all, human!

REMEMBER:

Great leadership means great results.

Contact us today if you would like to see real change in your focus, innovation and productivity.

sonia@soniamcdonald.com.au
sonia@leadershiphq.com.au
Phone – 1300 719 665
www.leadershiphq.com.au
www.soniamcdonald.com.au

Sonia
MCDONALD

Printed in Australia
AUHW021600080721
348355AU00011B/11